"For years, I have been studyir
biases, and so I picked up with .... book on the subject by social
psychologist Erin Devers. I learned something valuable and new on the first page,
and I finished the book as a fan of Professor Devers' work. If you want to be right
(as opposed to wrong) and you want to have valid reasons to feel good about
yourself, *The Unbiased Self* can really help you."
Brian D. McLaren, author of *Faith After Doubt* and *Do I Stay Christian?*

"*The Unbiased Self* explores the cognitive processes behind bias and the role of faith
in guiding individuals to confront and reduce these biases to achieve a more truthful
understanding of the self. The book is intellectually rigorous and spiritually en-
riching, and the result is a valuable resource for students, researchers, and practi-
tioners interested in the intersection of faith and psychology."
Joshua Clarkson, professor of marketing at the Lindner College of Business at the
University of Cincinnati

"From the first pages, *The Unbiased Self* convinced me that our dual needs—(1) to
be right and (2) to feel good about ourselves—drive cognitive bias! Dr. Devers
highlights how faith in God offers a more fulfilling way to meet these needs and
thus shed our biases. The book blends fascinating social psychology research with
relevant news stories and hilarious anecdotes. I found myself discussing its
central ideas with friends and family right away and implementing its practical
strategies to turn to God to 'hack' my thinking. Reading it, I felt joyous, grateful,
and deeply humbled!"
Ji Son, professor of psychology at Cal State LA

"Some books keep you to the end, and others long after. Dr. Devers presents us with
such a read—one that will have us turning pages for years after we close its covers.
But of course, I'm biased, having been a fan of her work for many years."
Jerry A. Pattengale, university professor at Indiana Wesleyan University

ERIN DEVERS

THE
UNBIASED
SELF

THE PSYCHOLOGY
OF OVERCOMING
COGNITIVE BIAS

*I may you will
l ove more generously
after reading!*

Erin Devers

ivp
Academic

An imprint of InterVarsity Press
Downers Grove, Illinois

InterVarsity Press
P.O. Box 1400 | Downers Grove, IL 60515-1426
ivpress.com | email@ivpress.com

InterVarsity Press® is the publishing division of InterVarsity Christian Fellowship/USA®. For more information, visit intervarsity.org.

All Scripture quotations, unless otherwise indicated, are taken from The Holy Bible, New International Version®, NIV®. Copyright © 1973, 1978, 1984, 2011 by Biblica, Inc.™ Used by permission of Zondervan. All rights reserved worldwide. www.zondervan.com. The "NIV" and "New International Version" are trademarks registered in the United States Patent and Trademark Office by Biblica, Inc.™

While any stories in this book are true, some names and identifying information may have been changed to protect the privacy of individuals.

The publisher cannot verify the accuracy or functionality of website URLs used in this book beyond the date of publication.

Cover design: David Fassett
Interior design: Daniel van Loon

ISBN 978-1-5140-0976-5 (print) | ISBN 978-1-5140-0977-2 (digital)

Printed in the United States of America ∞

Library of Congress Cataloging-in-Publication Data
A catalog record for this book is available from the Library of Congress.

31 30 29 28 27 26 25 | 13 12 11 10 9 8 7 6 5 4 3 2 1

CONTENTS

INTRODUCTION

WE WANT TO BE RIGHT AND WE WANT TO FEEL GOOD ABOUT OURSELVES

SINCE I BEGAN TEACHING SOCIAL PSYCHOLOGY in 2007, I have told students on each first day that social psychological research can help us explain approximately 95 percent of human behavior with one of two possible explanations. Students then proceed to quiz me on any number of strange human behaviors they have witnessed, with questions ranging from "Why did people storm the Capitol?" in the spring semester of 2021 to "Why did the Duggars decide to have so many kids?" My answer to the "Why do they do this?" question is either people truly believe they are doing the right thing,[1] or the behavior builds their self-esteem,[2] or sometimes both explanations contribute to the behavior.[3] I have students repeat, "We want to be right, and we want to feel good about ourselves," over and over during the course of the semester to remind them that these are the most common explanations for human behavior. These two motives contribute to bias, and recognizing these motives is the first step to

---

[1]Susan Fiske and Shelley Taylor, *Social Cognition*, 2nd ed. (New York: McGraw Hill, 1991); Richard E. Nisbett and Lee, *Human Inference: Strategies and Shortcomings of Human Judgment* (Englewood Cliffs, NJ: Prentice Hall, 1980).

[2]E. Aronson, "Dissonance, Hypocrisy, and the Self-Concept," in *Cognitive Dissonance Theory: Revival with Revisions and Controversies*, ed. E. Harmon-Jones and J. S. Mills (Washington, DC: American Psychological Association, 1998), 21-36; Mark R. Leary and Roy F. Baumeister, "The Nature and Function of Self-Esteem: Sociometer Theory," in *Advances in Experimental Social Psychology*, vol. 32, ed. Mark P. Zanna (San Diego, CA: Academic Press, 2000), 1-62.

[3]L. Festinger and E. Aronson, "The Arousal and Reduction of Dissonance in Social Contexts," in *Group Dynamics*, ed. Dorwin Cartwright and Alvin Zander (Evanston, IL: Row & Peterson, 1960), 214-31.

pursuing a less-biased self. Most students enter the class assuming that bias is something to do with racism and does not affect them, but bias, defined as systematic error in thinking,[4] is much broader than racism, and it affects all of us.

On one of my favorite podcasts, *Hidden Brain*, Shankar Vedantam shared the story of a young man who came from a rural part of Pennsylvania.[5] He had many advantages in childhood, but those advantages did not include a family history of Ivy League graduates. When he was accepted with early admission to Harvard University in the fall of 2016, it was life-changing good news for him and his parents. He received notoriety in his small town, and the possibilities that awaited him defied imagination.

When he was given the opportunity to meet his fellow classmates from Harvard's class of 2021 by participating in a group chat, he was eager to start making friends. This eagerness was in part fueled by his sense that he did not quite feel worthy of his admission or equal in caliber to the other students. His involvement in the main group chat of the new admits led to the sharing of memes. To get more validation from the other participants in the chat, the memes he and the other group members posted became more and more provocative and offensive over time. In retrospect this young man from rural Pennsylvania felt anxiety even when he was posting them because his eagerness to be liked was tinged with sick feelings of guilt. When Harvard got wind of the behavior in the group chat, the newly admitted students had their admissions revoked. Only by that time it was April, and the possibility of applying to other colleges had passed. The shock and sadness of the parents of these students was only paled by the depressed feelings experienced by the students themselves.

---

[4]Jennifer L. Eberhardt, *Biased: Uncovering the Hidden Prejudice That Shapes What We See, Think, and Do* (New York: Penguin, 2020), 6.
[5]Shankar Vedantam, "You Can't Hit Unsend," September 10, 2019, in *Hidden Brain*, NPR, podcast, https://hiddenbrain.org/podcast/you-cant-hit-unsend.

During class, I pause at this moment in the storytelling and ask my students to make predictions of what thoughts will pass through the mind of the rejected Harvard student from Pennsylvania. Many students think he will blame Harvard. Based on the pressure to maintain self-esteem, it would make sense to discount the severity of his behavior and blame Harvard. He can tell himself, "I am still a good person. There is something wrong with Harvard." In this case though, I urge the students to consider the magnitude of what happened and what would be the *best* way for this no-longer Ivy League student to think about this event.

Actually, the young man does not blame Harvard. He even says that if he had been a member of Harvard's admissions staff, he would have done the same thing. He learned that he needs other people to point out when he is making a mistake because he now knows that he is capable of making mistakes that have big consequences. He applied to colleges the next year and made the risky decision to include the description of his revoked admission to Harvard in his application essays. He applied to many Ivy League schools, and on the day that he was rejected from all of them, his parents came to show their support in the face of the bad news. He was accepted to a few colleges and was on the waitlist for one.

When he was finally admitted to a nearby school, his dad accompanied him on a campus visit. He and his dad were wandering in an academic building when they saw someone who was making copies. This man approached them to ask if they need help. When they described that they missed the tour, and only had until five to make a final decision on whether or not to enroll in the fall, the man took them into his office. The young man and the professor went on to have a deeply nerdy conversation about physics. The father describes that at one point in the conversation, the professor stopped, got down on his knees with clasped hands, and said, "Please, enroll here." In that moment, the father was nearly teary because after all the rejection and regret, someone saw the value in his son. When they got home from the visit, the father decided to send an email to the chair of the physics department to convey what a wonderful professor is in his department, only to find out that the man they had met was, in fact, the chair of the physics department.

What is the message of this story for my students and for us? We are all the Ivy League reject. The bias to feel good about ourselves leads all of us to do things that we regret later. We are sinners. We want to be liked as a quick boost to self-esteem, and sometimes we will do what is not right to get that boost. The beauty of the young man's story is that he learns several important things. He learns that he is vulnerable to bad behavior. Like him, we are all vulnerable and we are all susceptible to the bias that comes from wanting to feel good about ourselves. He also learns that he needs others to help slow down his thinking. We all need others to help slow down our thinking. We need others to help point us toward what is righteous especially when our self-esteem is on the line.

Many things may feel right in the moment, but we want to be righteous.[6] Beyond just reverting to the bias toward believing we are right, we should pursue accuracy. Just as we are all the Ivy League reject (some of us literally), we can all be that college professor. We are all given opportunities to look at others and restore their dignity. We can see them as God does, as beloved children. We can forgive much because we are forgiven much (Luke 7:47). We are the reject, and we can be the professor. *I hope that all my students can become less biased by figuring out a way to think and do what is righteous even when they must pay with their self-esteem. I hope you can too.*

---

[6]Jonathan Haidt, *The Righteous Mind: Why Good People Are Divided by Politics and Religion* (New York: Vintage, 2012), xiii.

ONE

THE ORIGINS OF BIAS

IF YOU WANT TO UNDERSTAND how to be less biased, you need to know what bias is. Cognitive bias is a "distorting lens"[1] or a *systematic* error in thinking.[2] In other words, cognitive bias is a built-in glitch in the system, something that prevents us from seeing the world accurately and ought to be a cause for concern. Cognitive biases provide an explanation for why two people from the same country, same city, or even the same household can interpret the same event very differently. Later on in this book, we will take a deeper dive into some of the specific biases, but first, we need to discuss the bias that precedes discussion of all the other biases: the bias blind spot.[3] The bias blind spot refers to the idea that people are really good at recognizing the biases of others but not their own. As you read this book, you will probably be able to generate your own examples of when you have witnessed the biases of others. You will hopefully laugh at the way others mistakenly interpret the world to serve their own ends. If this happens, and I hope it does, I will not have completely fulfilled the purpose of this book. The real purpose

---

[1] Jennifer L. Eberhardt, *Biased: Uncovering the Hidden Prejudice That Shapes What We See, Think, and Do* (New York: Penguin, 2020), 6.

[2] Amos Tversky and Daniel Kahneman, "Judgment Under Uncertainty: Heuristics and Biases; Biases in Judgments Reveal Some Heuristics of Thinking Under Uncertainty," *Science* 185, no. 4157 (1974): 1124.

[3] Emily Pronin, Daniel Y. Lin, and Lee Ross, "The Bias Blind Spot: Perceptions of Bias in Self Versus Others," *Personality and Social Psychology Bulletin* 28, no. 3 (2002): 370. The bias blind spot was named in reference to the visual blind spot where the optic nerve connects the eye to the brain.

of this book is not to increase your ability to notice the flaws in other people but to recognize and reduce your own bias.

The idea that we all want to believe that we are seeing the world as it truly is, a concept that psychologist Lee Ross calls naive realism,[4] is the cause of the bias blind spot. We do not always realize that there are gaps in the information we have. We do not know what we do not know.[5] For the most part, we are seeing the same landscapes and tasting the same foods as the people we share those experiences with, but our interpretations of the beauty or deliciousness of those experiences are not always the same. Most of us started to realize that people have different perspectives on the social world when we were around four years old.[6] In spite of this realization, many of us spend the rest of our lives believing that other people's different perspectives are less accurate than ours. This is naive realism. When we think hard, we can recognize that our social perceptions are different than other people's because social perception is incomplete. What do I mean when I write that social perception is incomplete? I mean that we do not get all the social information like a computer downloads a file; we only perceive the social information that we pay attention to, interpret, and then remember.[7] To pursue accuracy, to really understand and know what is true, we need to recognize and reduce our own biases. Knowing what the biases are is not enough.

When research on the bias blind spot emerged, researchers wondered whether thoughtful people might be able to recognize their

---

[4]Lee Ross and Andrew Ward, "Naive Realism in Everyday Life: Implications for Social Conflict and Misunderstanding," in *The Jean Piaget Symposium Series: Values and Knowledge*, ed. Edwin S. Reed, Elliot Turiel, and Terrance Brown (Mahwah, NJ: Lawrence Erlbaum Associates, 1996), 110-11.

[5]David Dunning, "The Dunning–Kruger Effect: On Being Ignorant of One's Own Ignorance," in *Advances in Experimental Social Psychology*, vol. 44 (San Diego, CA: Academic Press, 2011), 247-96.

[6]J. Perner and B. Lang, "Development of Theory of Mind and Executive Control," *Trends in Cognitive Sciences* 3, no. 9 (1999): 337-44.

[7]Hugh E. McDonald and Edward R. Hirt, "When Expectancy Meets Desire: Motivational Effects in Reconstructive Memory," *Journal of Personality and Social Psychology* 72, no. 1 (1997): 5-23.

own bias even if normal people could not.[8] So to identify the thoughtful people, whom they labeled "cognitively sophisticated," the researchers collected SAT scores, various personality measures related to cognition, and had people complete the cognitive reflection test.[9] The cognitive reflection test includes this question:

> A bat and a ball cost $1.10 in total. The bat costs $1.00 more than the ball. How much does the ball cost? ___ cents.

For most people, the first answer they come up with is ten cents. The right answer, which is five cents, requires more thought. Participants who spent time to get to the right answer on this type of question were labeled "cognitively sophisticated." The authors of the study hypothesized that the cognitively sophisticated participants (i.e., the thoughtful people) might be less susceptible to both cognitive biases and to the bias blind spot. What the researchers *found*, however, was that there was no correlation (and on some biases, a positive correlation) between scores on the measures of cognitive sophistication and both susceptibility to the biases and the bias blind spot; in fact, all participants demonstrated a susceptibility to bias and evidence of the bias blind spot.

Said another way, the thoughtful people were just as likely to be biased and just as likely to assume that other people are more biased than they are. The conclusion then is that most people are likely to fall prey to bias and are unlikely to recognize it in themselves even after being taught to recognize bias. The blind spot is in all our eyes. It explains why Jesus warned us that we often see the "speck" in our brother's eye yet "fail to see the plank" in our own eyes (Luke 6:41-42). The plank is in the blind spot. Therefore, rather than just informing

---

[8]Richard F. West, Russel J. Meserve, and Keith E. Stanovich, "Cognitive Sophistication Does Not Attenuate the Bias Blind Spot," *Journal of Personality and Social Psychology* 103, no. 3 (2012): 506-19.

[9]Shane Frederick, "Cognitive Reflection and Decision Making," *Journal of Economic Perspectives* 19, no. 4 (2005): 25-42.

readers about cognitive bias, this book will turn the spotlight away from judgments of the biases of others and *put the spotlight on the biases of the self.* In other words, we must try to "first take the plank" out of our own eyes (Luke 4:41-42). Before diving into the bias literature, it is important to understand how our desire to be right and feel good about ourselves contributes to bias.

WE WANT TO BE RIGHT

When I took Intro to Psychology as a college freshman, I was introduced to the analogy that our minds are like a room full of filing cabinets filled with the files that we have collected and organized throughout life. The file folders are called *schemas*,[10] but we often refer to them as concepts. These file folders are the way the mind organizes information and are the fundamental units of thinking. We are constantly opening the file folders and putting new information in them.[11] Imagine a baby encountering objects for the first time. When my oldest daughter started talking, she called dogs in the neighborhood "puppies." When she saw a bunny, she said "puppy." When she saw a kitten, she said "puppy." When she saw the weatherman on TV wearing a furry hat, she said "puppy." Anything that was furry and animated got labeled "puppy." This bias toward labeling everything a puppy mostly worked because puppies were the most frequent animal that my daughter encountered on walks in the neighborhood. Later, when she figured out that the weatherman wearing a furry hat was not a "puppy," she had to create a new file folder for "men wearing furry hats" that was separate from the "puppy" file folder. To avoid the bias of labeling everything "puppy," babies create new file folders for "kitties" and "bunnies." Eventually, older children can distinguish between many different animals and are mostly accurate in their identifications. Schemas help us navigate the world with increasing accuracy as we learn and mature in our thinking.

---

[10]Jean Piaget, *Le langage et la pensée chez l'enfant*, vol. 1 (Paris: Delachaux and Niestlé, 1923).
[11]Frederic C. Bartlett, *Remembering* (Cambridge: Cambridge University Press, 1932).

WE WANT TO BE RIGHT SO WE COLLECT
AND ORGANIZE FILE FOLDERS

As we develop and increase our exposure to a variety of domains, including those not having to do with animals, we create a filing system that is increasingly accurate, diversified, and less biased. Imagine that now in adulthood, your mind is a room that has been curated by someone who has gone to the Container Store and has organized everything in a manner worthy of an organizational TV show episode. There is a color-coding system, and all of the containers are easily identifiable and accessible. There are schemas for each person we meet, schemas for groups (otherwise known as stereotypes), schemas for events, and a self-schema. *The purpose of creating this beautiful room is so that you can be right.*[12] When someone asks us about something, we go to the container containing the appropriate file folder and pull out our answer—our correct answer. What we don't realize in using our beautiful filing systems is that some information is missing. It doesn't *feel* like anything is missing because our filing rooms appear to have everything; however, it is not possible to become experts in every domain (only God's mind has complete information), which means that in some situations, we may be relying on an incomplete file folder that we don't recognize is incomplete. Like a visual blind spot, we don't see the blind spot in our files. If someone asked us to point to our visual blind spots, we could not do it. There are missing pieces in our fields of vision that our brains fill in, and there are missing pieces in our available information that our brains fill in.[13] I will give a few examples to make the connection between schemas and bias.

---

[12]To make sure we are speaking the same psychological language, consider that "right" in this context refers to accuracy. I would extend this definition to include "righteous," and there is considerable evidence to suggest that people are not only motivated to be righteous but to view themselves as more moral than others. See Scott T. Allison, David M. Messick, and George R. Goethals, "On Being Better but Not Smarter Than Others: The Muhammad Ali Effect," *Social Cognition* 7, no. 3 (1989): 275-95.

[13]Mahzarin R. Banaji and Anthony G. Greenwald, *Blindspot: Hidden Biases of Good People* (New York: Bantam, 2016), xi-xiii.

Let's compare what happens in a kindergarten classroom over the course of a day when you bring in a novice compared to an expert substitute teacher. Imagine a new substitute teacher in a kindergarten classroom for the first time. She has had limited experience with children so her file folder for "kindergarteners" is based on a few interactions she had with a younger cousin. Right now, she doesn't even know what she doesn't know about kindergartners, so when she walks into a room full of kindergarteners, she assumes these kids will be like her cousin. Her cousin was a good reader but was not yet potty trained, so she spends a lot of time taking kids to the bathroom and very little time on phonics. It is likely that over the course of the day a lot of mistakes were made and a lot of time was wasted. It is likely that the children did not learn very much, but everyone's pants stayed dry.

Contrast that with a seasoned kindergarten teacher, with a large file folder for "kindergarteners," who not only knows what students are supposed to learn in kindergarten but can even identify possible challenges a particular child might be struggling with in the course of a short interaction. This seasoned teacher can jump in right away and invite students to start learning. Even though her file folder is nearly complete, she does not know each individual child so she will have to rely heavily on her past interactions with other kindergarteners. Relying on a file folder that is full and mostly complete will occasionally lead to errors but fewer errors than for the novice substitute teacher. The experienced teacher will likely expect that all kindergarteners will be potty trained. She will mostly be right. She will be surprised if one wets his pants. (Having the "mind of God" would have made it clear which child was not potty trained.) The mostly complete file folder was correct in predicting that most kindergarteners are potty trained. Therefore, the substitute teacher did not need to focus a lot of attention on it, but unexpected and sometimes unpleasant exceptions may occur. It is likely that the kindergarteners learned a lot from the seasoned teacher, but a bathroom-related accident was not out of the realm of possibility.

When we compare the performance of these two teachers, neither one of them had all the information necessary to make the day run *perfectly* with kindergarteners. The experienced teacher had a lot more information to help her prioritize her attention, whereas the inexperienced teacher relied on limited information that made it difficult for her to do little more than babysit. If we consider the importance of learning to read, we recognize that there is a significant cost to occasionally being wrong about kindergarteners.[14]

Let me give you another more gruesome and harrowing example. Imagine being selected to serve on a jury and hear the story of a woman who was raped and brutalized while jogging in a local park. The pictures are appalling. It is horrifying that anyone would do this to someone in your community. The defendant reads the confession he gave. There is no physical evidence linking him to the crime, but the confession is detailed and compelling and mostly accurate to the facts of the case. Someone should pay for the crime to bring justice to the woman and her family. Most people would have convicted the young man who confessed. Most people's file folder for "guilty people" includes the idea that if a person confesses to a crime, that person must be guilty. In the absence of evidence that someone else is guilty, it makes sense to think that the person who confessed is guilty even if there is not much physical evidence to support the conviction.

It turns out that many people, including most people who work in law enforcement, believe that only guilty people would confess to a crime. Many jurors are very likely to convict anyone who confesses even if no compelling physical evidence is presented. This is exactly what happened to the jurors on the cases of the Central Park Five.[15] Each of the five teenagers who were convicted in the brutal attack of

---

[14]Emily Hanford, "Why Millions of Kids Can't Read and What Better Teaching Can Do About It," January 2, 2019, NPR, www.npr.org/2019/01/02/677722959/why-millions-of-kids-cant-read-and-what-better-teaching-can-do-about-it.

[15]Lauren Cook, "Central Park Five: What to Know About the Jogger Rape Case," June 5, 2019, AMNY, www.amny.com/news/central-park-five-1-19884350.

Trisha Meili in the spring of 1989 gave detailed confessions. In 2002, DNA evidence revealed that none of those teenagers were involved; rather, Trisha was attacked by one man, Matias Reyes. The members of the Central Park Five received a $41 million settlement. The cost of a bias caused by an inaccurate file folder for "guilty people" was steep for all involved. Jurors, like a substitute kindergarten teacher, must rely on a limited "guilty" file folder even if they do not have all the information that would be helpful to make an accurate decision. None of us are immune to this kind of inaccuracy; we all use our schemas to fill in the missing information of our blind spots.

Hopefully, it makes us feel uncomfortable to think that we could have made the same kind of mistake as the jurors for the Central Park Five. This uncomfortable feeling is there because we want to pursue accuracy and righteousness. The beautiful room full of file folders was created to help us believe we are right, but if the information in the file folder is incomplete, we might not realize it, and then bias will go unchecked. The jurors in the cases of the Central Park Five did not have a complete file folder for the specific cases because there was a lot of missing evidence, and their file folders for "guilty people" did not include the conditions under which a false confession is likely. At the time of the original convictions, it is likely that the jurors believed they were right. *In this book, we will make a distinction between feeling right and pursuing accuracy.* Wanting to be right leads us to rely on our incomplete file folders without checking for bias. Pursuing accuracy involves considering what information might be missing from the file folders before rendering a judgment. Recognizing the *incompleteness* of the content of the file folders is one step toward recognizing our own bias.

WE WANT TO BE RIGHT SO WE USE OUR SCHEMAS TO FILTER INFORMATION

Our desire to be right motivated us to create the organized room of incomplete file folders, and it guides the processing of new information.

Bias emerges not only because we are missing information in file folders, but because the information we put into the file folders passes through the filter of our filing system. For example, many people experience that when they decide to buy a particular car, they see it everywhere. This is called the Baader-Meinhof phenomenon.[16] The effect got its name when a person on a message board in 1994 started writing about how having once read about the German terrorist group, Baader-Meinhof, he started noticing more and more references to it. Given the obscurity of a terrorist organization that was active in the 1970s, this was curious. Other people on the message board started posting their experiences of having read something for the first time and then noticing it everywhere. The explanation given by psychologists for this phenomenon is that it is the result of selective attention.[17] *Once we have activated a schema, that schema guides our attention and filters our experiences.*

In an experiment, imagine you are told to read the following story about newlyweds who are considering their first home purchase and are told to try to remember as many details about the house as possible. The story reads,

> The time came for them to go to the house. No one was in sight, so they decided to examine the house carefully from the outside. They looked carefully at the front of the house and noticed that the paint on the porch was beginning to peel. They walked around the side and looked through the windows into the spacious living room. The room was luxuriously furnished. The owners had arranged the furniture to orient toward a television with a large screen. A VCR and a new stereo completed the entertainment center. The living room was split-level, and going down three stairs, there was a vast stone fireplace. In front of this was a sofa and a coffee table, on top of which sat a laptop computer. A sliding glass door in the back wall

---

[16]Kate Kershner and Austin Henderson, "What's the Baader-Meinhof Phenomenon?," September 5, 2023, HowStuffWorks, https://science.howstuffworks.com/life/inside-the-mind/human-brain/baader-meinhof-phenomenon.htm.

[17]William A. Johnston and Veronica J. Dark, "Selective Attention," *Annual Review of Psychology* 37, no. 1 (1986): 43-75.

opened to an outside patio. They then went around the other side of the house. The first room they saw was the dining room, which was big enough to house a table for eight. A cabinet on one side held crystal, china, and silverware. Despite this evidence of luxury, the wallpaper appeared yellowed and faded.[18]

Consider what a person might remember having just read that paragraph. Most people who do this remember the VCR because of its anachronistic qualities but also notice things like the large rooms and stone fireplace. In a different version of this experiment, participants are asked to read the same paragraph about the house but are told that two burglars are considering robbing the house instead of being told that newlyweds are considering buying the house. The people who read the burglar version pay more attention to the computer, crystal, and TV. People in both conditions remembered an equal number of things, but the things they remembered were different. In both versions, everyone is trying to remember things accurately, but they have different file folders open and are not able to remember every detail no matter what version they read.

This happens in real life frequently. Consider meeting someone for the first time. We *pay attention to different information* when we meet someone we are interviewing for a job compared to when we meet that same someone as a potential brother-in-law. In both cases, being a hard worker is important, but attractiveness might matter more in the case of marrying a superficial sister. We ask different questions and *draw different conclusions* depending on whether the "future family member" file is open or if the "temporary desk worker" file is open. After the interview is over, we *remember different things* about the person depending on whether they are about to marry into our family or not. Neither of these file folders is likely to be more accurate than the other, but the file folders will be different, and lead

[18]Jerry Zadny and Harold B. Gerard, "Attributed Intentions and Informational Selectivity," *Journal of Experimental Social Psychology* 10, no. 1 (1974): 34-52.

to a different bias. None of the folders can be completely accurate because they are not complete. It is impossible to store all the information about a person or situation. The lack of completeness in our file folders means that there is bias. It reflects the limits of our perception. We can try to be as accurate as possible but must recognize that bias creeps in because the knowledge in our file folders is incomplete, and our filing system is filtering out information that might be important. If the person we interviewed is applying for a job, and we use the "future family member" folder, we will not end up with the right information.

In a similar experiment, a group of college students participated in what they were told was an experiment about "teacher evaluation methods."[19] In the experiment, the participants were introduced to Hannah, who they were told was in the fourth grade. In the control condition, they were asked to evaluate her academic capabilities but were not given any information other than her socioeconomic status (either that she was rich or poor). In the experimental condition, participants found out her socioeconomic status, but also watched a video of her taking a twenty-five-item achievement test. She missed some of the easy problems and did well on some difficult problems. All the participants were asked to judge her academic capabilities.

The participants were well-meaning college students who wanted to treat Hannah fairly without using her parent's financial status to infer how smart she was. The participants who did not watch the video of Hannah taking the test, but did know whether she was rich or poor, did what you would expect people who are trying to be unbiased to do. If she is in fourth grade, she is probably typical for a fourth grader. There was not a difference in the ratings of academic capabilities for the rich versus poor version of Hannah. The interesting part of the experiment is revealed by the participants in

---

[19]John M. Darley and Paget H. Gross, "A Hypothesis-Confirming Bias in Labeling Effects," *Journal of Personality and Social Psychology* 44, no. 1 (1983): 20-33.

the experimental condition. Only when they get to watch the video of Hannah taking the test do the participants give higher ratings to the rich Hannah. They judge her as being nearly equivalent to a fifth grader. When participants watched the video of poor Hannah, they judged her as being equivalent to a third grader.

Let's consider what was happening in the minds of the participants in the experimental condition. It is likely that before watching the video, those participants were trying to avoid assuming that poor Hannah is less capable. The file folder for "rich kids" and "poor kids" was open, but it did not impact the judgments until more information was given. In a memory test after the experiment, participants who watched the video of rich Hannah take the test were more likely to remember the difficult questions she answered correctly, and students who watched the video of poor Hannah take the test were more likely to remember the easy questions that she missed. The bottom line of this experiment is that even when people want to avoid using a bias, the schema *guides attention* toward the information that is consistent with the schema.

File folders that are chronically open not only guide attention in one situation but *create the lens* by which new information is filtered. The lens over time creates a worldview. This idea is communicated by a famous C. S. Lewis quote: "I believe in Christianity as I believe that the sun has risen: not only because I see it, but because by it I see everything else."[20] Having chronically activated file folders facilitates one of the most pernicious biases, confirmation bias.

Confirmation bias is the tendency to take in and interpret information in such a way that it confirms rather than challenges what we already think.[21] The desire to be right motivates us to look for evidence

---

[20]C. S. Lewis, *They Asked for a Paper* (London: Geoffrey Bles, 1962). Lewis was not making an argument to avoid disconfirming information, but this quote reveals how a worldview can shape information.

[21]Raymond S. Nickerson, "Confirmation Bias: A Ubiquitous Phenomenon in Many Guises," *Review of General Psychology* 2, no. 2 (1998): 175.

in the world of what we already believe. This is why we might select a particular news outlet or talk about certain topics with certain friends who we know already agree with us. The world is easier to navigate when we do not have to question things. There is an obvious downside to confirmation bias—it can keep us stuck in a wrong way of thinking.

As in the example of the Central Park Five, most people believe that no one would confess to a crime unless they were guilty. If we are like most people and hold this belief, we are likely to use the confession to draw our conclusion: the defendant is guilty. After drawing that conclusion, the confirmation bias suggests that all new information regarding the evidence will be interpreted to confirm rather than challenge that the defendant is guilty. To test this, psychologists Jeff Kukucka and Saul Kassin had participants complete an online experiment in which they all read a story, based on a real case, in which a bank robber gave a handwritten note to the bank teller, robbed the bank, and managed to escape.[22] Next, the police were able to capture someone resembling the description given by the bank teller, who then wrote a waiver of his Miranda rights by hand before being questioned. In the confession conditions, participants found out that the suspect confessed, but then later recanted by claiming that the confession was coerced. Participants in the non-confession condition were told that the suspect never wavered in his claim of innocence the entire time. Next all participants were given a copy of the handwritten note (originally given to the bank teller) and the handwritten waiver of Miranda rights to judge whether or not both were written by the defendant. For half of the participants, the handwriting was very similar for both notes. For the other half of the participants, the handwriting was not similar. Participants who were told that the suspect confessed were more likely to perceive a match

---

[22]Jeff Kukucka and Saul M. Kassin, "Do Confessions Taint Perceptions of Handwriting Evidence? An Empirical Test of the Forensic Confirmation Bias," *Law and Human Behavior* 38, no. 3 (2014): 256-70.

in the handwriting than participants who were told the suspect maintained his innocence regardless of the actual similarity of the handwriting. The participants confirmed in the handwriting what they already believed about the guilt of the suspect. To avoid confirmation bias and pursue accuracy (not just feeling right), we must be vigilant about seeking disconfirming information.

In addition to the specific filters that our particular schemas create, our brains have a shared filter that favors negative content.[23] We have a well-documented *negativity bias* in how we take in information.[24] It extends to how we form impressions of others, memory, perception, and decision-making.[25] In a compelling experiment, participants were asked to make judgments about the truth of various claims that were either given a positive or negative frame. For example, half of participants in an experiment were told that "85% of attempted instances of rape were successful," while the other half were told that "15% of attempted instances of rape were unsuccessful."[26] Participants were more likely to believe that the first more negative framing of the information was true, even though the facts of the sentences are the same. Both optimists and pessimists were more likely to believe the negatively framed statements than the positively framed ones.

News organizations and social media exploit and expose the negativity bias. Negative information drives engagement on social media and in news. Specifically, moral outrage and negative content about a rival group increases the probability that something will get shared on social media.[27] In the past few years, researchers have found that

[23]Catherine J. Norris, "The Negativity Bias, Revisited: Evidence from Neuroscience Measures and an Individual Differences Approach," *Social Neuroscience* 16, no. 1(2021): 68-82.

[24]Interestingly, this effect has recently been demonstrated to decline with age. Laura L. Carstensen and Marguerite DeLiema, "The Positivity Effect: A Negativity Bias in Youth Fades with Age," *Current Opinion in Behavioral Sciences* 19 (2018): 7-12.

[25]Paul Rozin and Edward B. Royzman, "Negativity Bias, Negativity Dominance, and Contagion," *Personality and Social Psychology Review* 5, no. 4 (2001): 296-320.

[26]Benjamin E. Hilbig, "Sad, Thus True: Negativity Bias in Judgments of Truth," *Journal of Experimental Social Psychology* 45, no. 4 (July 2009): 983-86.

[27]Steve Rathje, Jay J. Van Bavel, and Sander van der Linden, "Out-Group Animosity Drives

if a liberal mentions moral outrage and the word "conservative" or "republican" it will get more attention than mentioning positive information or the success of a fellow liberal. You can then imagine if humans are set up to pay attention to negative news, and our capitalistic culture knows how to provide it for us, then we are going to get caught in a confirmation bias web. This web leads us to conclude that many negative things are happening and that we are not equipped to solve problems because they are presented as being worse than they actually are. To use an analogy, if we think about the effect of naturally occurring negativity bias as a hit of caffeine, it is at the level of green tea. The level of hit we get from social media is like the hit you get from energy drinks that can kill us if consumed at high volume. This negativity bias-driven thought cycle reflects a disconnection from what is true. When we are caught in a web of confirmation bias, we get the benefit of feeling right, but we are no longer pursuing accuracy.

DON'T THINK ABOUT A WHITE BEAR. Try not to think about a white bear for the next sixty seconds. If you are like the participants in Wegner's study, you found "not thinking about a white bear" to be a difficult task.[28] To be even remotely successful at the task, a person should focus on thinking about something else like a grocery list or a pink bear. Trying not to think about negative things is just as difficult as trying not to think about a white bear. So instead of simply not thinking about negative things, the better advice is to try to think about the things that are true, lovely, noble, and of good report (see Philippians 4:8). When I pray for my daughters each day before they head off to school, I pray that their attention will be directed to what is true and delightful. The negativity bias is so pronounced that more

---

Engagement on Social Media," *Proceedings of the National Academy of Sciences* 118, no. 26 (June 23, 2021): 1-9.

[28]Daniel M. Wegner, "Ironic Processes of Mental Control," *Psychological Review 101*, no. 1 (1994): 34-52, https://doi.org/10.1037/0033-295x.101.1.34.

than just combatting negative information with positive information, this book will help us pursue what is accurate and avoid bias.

WE WANT TO BE RIGHT AND EFFICIENT

So far, it might seem advantageous to try to avoid schemas and file folders altogether because they introduce bias, but even if that were possible, trying to function without an organized thought structure would be like a return to infancy but without the infant's cute factor. We need our organized filing system to help us pursue accuracy even if the side effect of the filing system is bias. We don't have time to collect all the information to complete our filing system, and schemas help us to function in the world without complete knowledge. I presented this earlier as a disadvantage and source of bias; but on the other hand, schemas save us time. *Schemas help us behave efficiently in the world without having to give attention and mental resources to every stimulus.* The efficiency of schemas is best characterized in the use of cognitive heuristics. Heuristics are "rules of thumb" that work well most of the time, but not all the time. Kahneman and Tversky, pioneers of the study of bias and heuristics, began by identifying rules of thumb like the representativeness heuristic, in which people make probability judgments based on similarity and ignore basic facts.[29] For example, my husband is convinced there is a bobcat that lives in our neighborhood because the animal he sees in our backyard looks very similar to a bobcat. If we still lived in California, it would be likely he is right since many bobcats live in California. Given the number of bobcats that live in northern Indiana, I'm going to continue believing that he saw a large cat in our backyard, not a bobcat. He is using similarity to "categorize the bobcat" and ignoring the low probability that bobcats live here. This "rule of thumb" that involves using similarity to cat-

---

[29]Daniel Kahneman and Amos Tversky, "Subjective Probability: A Judgment of Representativeness," *Cognitive Psychology* 3, no. 3 (1972): 430-454.

egorize things usually works pretty well. If it looks like a duck, and quacks like a duck, it is probably a duck, unless you live in Antarctica. Only when the base rate for something is low, like ducks in Antarctica or bobcats in northern Indiana, does the representativeness heuristic lead to error.

Heuristics are generally useful because they help us to be efficient thinkers and decision makers. Some people are less willing than others to employ heuristics. Psychologists have developed personality scales to measure a person's desire to maximize. Maximizers will not settle for the second-best decision but will research every possible angle before zeroing in on the best decision regardless of how much time is required. Maximizers do not ask the question, "Is this a *good* outcome?" Instead, they ask, "Is this the *best* outcome?"[30] Satisficers, on the other hand, are sensitive to the time-accuracy trade-off and are willing to sacrifice the best outcome to save time. They are willing to accept a good outcome without being sure that it is the best outcome. Satisficers employ more heuristics. When a satisficer goes to the grocery, they don't need to know if they could have gotten better, cheaper, or more locally sourced produce at a competing grocery. They are buying the first available version that meets the recipe requirements. Not surprisingly, satisficers are happier, more optimistic, have higher self-esteem, and are more satisfied with their lives than maximizers.[31] Heuristics save us time and contribute to happiness, but they are a cause of bias. Satisficers are willing to make the time-accuracy trade-off in favor of time with a potential loss of accuracy; given the limits of available time, we all must satisfice sometimes.

In addition to the use of heuristics, there are other ways that our thinking works in service of efficiency. Cognitive and social psychologists have developed dual-process models to explain that there are two

---

[30]Barry Schwartz et al., "Maximizing Versus Satisficing: Happiness Is a Matter of Choice," *Journal of Personality and Social Psychology* 83, no. 5 (2002): 1178-97.
[31]Schwartz et al., "Maximizing Versus Satisficing."

ways of thinking and remembering information.[32] The first way, system one processing, is thinking that is referred to as fast or automatic. Automatic (fast) thinking happens below awareness, is unintentional, is outside of human control, and is *efficient*.[33] This constellation of features is also referred to as implicit thinking. In contrast, system two processing is thinking that is slow or controlled. Controlled (slow) thinking is effortful, intentional, occurs above awareness, and is time consuming. This is what most non-psychologists refer to as "thinking." It is referred to by psychologists as explicit thinking. This distinction between fast and slow, automatic and controlled, explicit and implicit, is one of the most important distinctions for the purposes of understanding thinking and reducing bias. More examples are coming, but for now, it might be helpful to think of automatic processing like the thinking it takes to drive a car under normal conditions in familiar neighborhoods, but controlled processing is the thinking it takes to drive on the opposite side of the road in an unfamiliar city.

Perhaps because of Freud's insistence that the unconscious is full of sublimated sexual desires,[34] implicit, fast, automatic thinking has gotten a bad reputation. As a culture, we exalt the rational, logical, explicit, pro/con list-making thinking that looks more like controlled thinking. However, bias can exist in both automatic and controlled thinking. Returning to the research on the bias blind spot, which demonstrates that people are better at seeing the bias in others than themselves, the researchers began by making the argument that bias largely exists in fast thinking. They hypothesized that if you make people aware of the bias, they can use their controlled thinking to correct the bias. There is some evidence, which I will discuss later, that this can

[32]Shelly Chaiken and Yaacov Trope, *Dual-Process Theories in Social Psychology* (New York: Guilford Press, 1999).

[33]J. Bargh, "The Four Horsemen of Automaticity: Awareness, Efficiency, Intentions and Control," in *Handbook of Social Cognition*, vol. 1, ed. Thomas K. Srull and Robert S. Wyer, 2nd ed. (Hillsdale, NJ: Lawrence Erlbaum, 1994), 1-40.

[34]Mick Power and Chris R. Brewin, "From Freud to Cognitive Science: A Contemporary Account of the Unconscious," *British Journal of Clinical Psychology* 30, no. 4 (1991): 289-310.

work to reduce some biases when people are motivated to pursue accuracy and have sufficient mental resources.[35] However, as in the example of the bias blind spot, even people who were practiced at overriding their initial automatic response to correctly use controlled thinking to answer questions regarding the price of balls and bats,[36] were not able to avoid biased responses and believed that they were less susceptible to bias than other people.[37] However, logic holds that since automatic thinking occurs below awareness and personal control, controlled thinking must be employed to reduce the bias that results from both controlled and automatic thinking. Logic also holds that automatic thinking, given that it exists below awareness, is more difficult to pinpoint; thus, bias that emerges from our efficient fast thinking is hard to correct. So far, the cause of bias that we have been discussing is rooted in cognitive explanations such as the incompleteness of schemas, the way schemas guide our attention, and the efficiency of our thinking. These features of cognition that are guided by a desire to feel right are important to developing an understanding of bias. However, they don't explain some of the ridiculous human behavior we observe on a regular basis. Given enough motivation to pursue accuracy (not just feeling right), it might be possible to reduce bias, but there is another important motive that gets in the way of accuracy.

WE WANT TO FEEL GOOD ABOUT OURSELVES

Imagine you are in a lab where you have been told that your cognitive aptitude will be assessed.[38] In your first task you are told to unscramble a series of letters to form words, a task the experimenters

---

[35]Daniel T. Gilbert, "Inferential Correction," in *Heuristics and Biases: The Psychology of Intuitive Judgment*, ed. Thomas Gilovich, Dale W. Griffin, and Daniel Kahneman (New York: Cambridge University Press, 2002), 167-84, https://doi.org/10.1017/CBO9780511808098.011.

[36]Frederick, "Cognitive Reflection and Decision Making."

[37]West, Meserve, and Stanovich, "Cognitive Sophistication Does Not Attenuate the Bias Blind Spot."

[38]Steven Berglas and Edward E. Jones, "Drug Choice as a Self-Handicapping Strategy in Response to Noncontingent Success," *Journal of Personality and Social Psychology* 36, no. 4 (1978): 405-17, https://doi.org/10.1037//0022-3514.36.4.405.

have designed to be impossible. You spend about twenty minutes trying to unscramble the words but have little success. If anything, you feel you have failed the task. Then an experimenter comes in, looks at your work, and tells you that you have performed very well, even brilliantly compared to past participants. If you are like most participants in this experiment who receive this feedback, you are feeling confused. Then the experimenter gives you an option to take one of two drugs before attempting the next task. One of the drugs is likely to enhance performance and one is likely to impair performance. To most people who are not in this experiment, it seems like an easy choice. Why would anyone take a drug that impairs performance in the middle of an assessment of cognitive aptitude? Turns out 70 percent of the male participants who had just received the unsettling, positive feedback about their performance on the unsolvable anagram task chose to take the drug that would impair performance. This is compared to 13 percent of male participants who were in the condition in which the anagrams were solvable and thus the positive feedback appears warranted.

What is the reason for taking the performance-impairing drug? The desire to be right could not explain why a person would take a drug to impair their own performance. In addition to wanting to be right, *we want to feel good about ourselves.* This motive is at play in the decision to take the performance-impairing drug. Taking the performance-impairing drug creates a built-in excuse for poor performance on the next task. Taking the performance-impairing drug allows the participant to tell himself, "I am brilliant, just like the experimenter said, but my failure on the second task was caused by the drug, not by my low cognitive aptitude."

That anyone would choose to impair their performance may seem hard to believe but consider that the same phenomenon is likely one explanation for why people procrastinate on important tasks. If a person waits until the last minute to write a paper, the poor grade on the paper could be explained by the last-minute rush and not by the student's overall inability to write a good paper. In the mind of the student, self-esteem is preserved. "I could have written a good paper, if only I hadn't procrastinated." The translation of this could be, "My poor grade is not a reflection of my low ability. I am still a good student." We know that procrastination leads to a poorer outcome so why do we do it? We agree with Paul's words, "I do not understand what I do. For what I want to do I do not do, but what I hate I do" (Romans 7:15). We do things like tell white lies, eat gluttonously, scroll social media, and exaggerate our performance when we ought to know better. We want to feel good about ourselves even when it costs us something like seeing the world accurately or getting a good grade on a paper.

The behavior described in the performance-impairing drug experiment is called "self-handicapping," which is defined as setting up explanations in advance of poor performance to protect self-esteem.[39] Men tend to self-handicap by withdrawing effort, like when they stop trying to repair a relationship, skip sports practice, or avoid studying for an important test. Women tend to do it by giving an excuse like, "I might not do well because I am tired/sick/anxious." Women rarely withdraw effort as a self-handicapping strategy. Self-handicapping, especially the kind that involves withdrawing effort, not surprisingly leads to worse outcomes. If my students don't study for tests, they do worse. If humans were rational actors who were pursuing accuracy, they would not self-handicap. Self-handicapping happens because we want to feel good about ourselves. In a follow-up study to the drug study described above, participants were more likely to take the drug that impairs performance when they believed that the experimenter would know which drug they chose and their score on the test.[40] This

---

[39]Berglas and Jones, "Drug Choice as a Self-Handicapping Strategy in Response to Noncontingent Success."

[40]Thomas A. Kolditz and Robert M. Arkin, "An Impression Management Interpretation of the Self-Handicapping Strategy," *Journal of Personality and Social Psychology* 43, no. 3 (1982): 492-502, https://doi.org/10.1037/0022-3514.43.3.492.

demonstrates that part of our desire to maintain self-esteem is rooted in what we think others think of us. We feel good about ourselves when we think other people think well of us.

If pursuing accuracy was the primary motivation people held, the world would be a more wonderful place. This motive would be prompting people to create file folders with as much accurate information as possible, to take their time considering the lens created by the file folders, and to seek out disconfirming information. Imagine how much easier it would be to solve problems if we could trust that everyone was only using near-complete file folders to give us accurate information. People's behavior would be rational and predictable. Unfortunately, wanting to feel good through maintaining self-esteem will complicate the quest for truth. Instead of behaving rationally, people *rationalize* to maintain self-esteem. Self-esteem refers to a global evaluation of self-worth,[41] which is a personal judgment that is not necessarily based on accomplishments. Given that a global evaluation of self-worth does not require undeniable evidence of successful performance, it is easy and advantageous to filter information through the lens of self-esteem; thus, *the motive to maintain self-esteem causes bias.* We will trade accuracy and righteousness for good feelings and self-esteem. Often, like a self-handicapper, we will lie to others and even to ourselves to save face because acknowledging major deficiencies in ourselves is very difficult.

Data suggests that depressed people are more accurate in their assessments of the causes of other people's behavior than are non-depressed people.[42] People are less depressed when they misrepresent information in service of self-esteem.[43] People who are not

---

[41]Brett W. Pelham and William B. Swann, "From Self-Conceptions to Self-Worth: On the Sources and Structure of Global Self-Esteem," *Journal of Personality and Social Psychology* 57, no. 4 (1989): 672-80.

[42]Kerry L. Marsh and Gifford Weary, "Depression and Attributional Complexity," *Personality and Social Psychology Bulletin* 15, no. 3 (1989): 325-36.

[43]Mark R. Leary and Roy F. Baumeister, "The Nature and Function of Self-Esteem: Sociometer Theory," in *Advances in Experimental Social Psychology*, vol. 32, ed. Mark P. Zanna (San Diego, CA: Academic Press, 2000), 1-62.

putting effort into spinning the information using strategies like self-handicapping to benefit their self-esteem are more likely to be depressed.[44] This finding is very ironically depressing to me. In an adaptation of Oscar Wilde's play, the lead character accurately states, "It takes a great deal of courage to see the world in all its tainted glory and still to love it."[45] Maybe it takes courage to see the world accurately because the consequence is depression. To avoid this depression, many of us choose to see the world through rose-colored glasses.

As I was getting to know a student of mine, she began to share many of the personal details of her life. She told me about her Christian upbringing, including the message she received from her church and her parents surrounding the importance of sexual purity, and how deeply she had internalized this message. She then went on to describe how in high school she and her boyfriend were sexually active, but she only realized that what they were doing was sex later. At the time that they were sexually active, she was so committed to seeing herself as sexually pure that she figured out a way to convince herself that what she was doing was not sex. If I had not witnessed the sincerity of her story firsthand, I would not have believed this story. The only way to make sense of her story is to understand that the power of wanting to feel good about ourselves can prevent us from seeing things accurately. It made her feel good to think of herself as a good Christian girl, and if a good Christian girl does not have premarital sex, she had two choices, and both options would require her to change her file folders. One choice would be to change the "self" file folder and conclude that she was not a good Christian girl, and she would have to deal with the negative feelings of not being good or of not being Christian. Her other choice was to change the sex file folder by recategorizing what she was doing as "not sex." Choosing to recategorize her behavior as "not sex"

---

[44]Howard Tennen and Sharon Herzberger, "Depression, Self-Esteem, and the Absence of Self-Protective Attributional Biases," *Journal of Personality and Social Psychology* 52, no. 1 (1987): 72.

[45]*An Ideal Husband*, directed by Oliver Parker (Santa Monica, CA: Icon Productions, 1999).

was not accurate (or righteous), but it allowed her to keep on feeling like a good Christian girl. It was easier on her self-esteem to change the "sex" file folder than change the way she thought about herself.

I tell this story to point out the extremes to which a person can go to maintain a positive self-view, but we are all doing this on smaller scales every time we tell a white lie or participate in hazing. Hazing, the embarrassing non-life-threatening kind, is a helpful tactic to increase commitment to a group. If you work hard to join a group either through effort or having to wear an embarrassing hat, you will value the group more because of the pressure to resolve the tension in the motives to be right and to feel good about yourself.[46] Let's say you have to sing a children's song loudly in a public place while pushing a doll in a stroller in order to be accepted into a group. You will likely think to yourself, "Singing songs in public when people are trying to drink coffee in peace is not the right thing to do and is generally embarrassing to me." To justify the action to feel good about yourself, you have to rationalize, "Joining this group makes this embarrassing behavior worth it." Likewise, if you must go through an extensive vetting process to get a boring, unfulfilling job, you are likely to value the job and stick with it longer than if you were hired based on simply submitting a resume online.

It is much easier to find a way to justify or rationalize a behavior than it is to grapple with the truth of our own poor judgment or immoral behavior.[47] We are expert rationalizers who can justify our behavior automatically without realizing we are doing it.[48] We do not want to file information in memory that threatens how we characterize our behavior as smart and moral. The tension of not living up to our beliefs is real. Participants who eat beef jerky rate the moral

---

[46]Elliot Aronson and Judson Mills, "The Effect of Severity of Initiation on Liking for a Group," *The Journal of Abnormal and Social Psychology* 59, no. 2 (1959): 177-81.

[47]Harold B. Gerard and Grover C. Mathewson, "The Effects of Severity of Initiation on Liking for a Group: A Replication," *Journal of Experimental Social Psychology* 2, no. 3 (1966): 278-87.

[48]Jake Quilty-Dunn, "Rationalization Is Irrational and Self-Serving, but Useful," *Behavioral and Brain Sciences* 43 (2020).

status of cows as lower than the participants who are randomly assigned to eat dried nuts.[49] Participants who shock other students in the course of an experiment feel the need to denigrate those students.[50] Rather than admitting that we behaved poorly, *it is easier to blame the victim.* More frequently than I am even aware, I blame my poor behavior on the people around me, which increases the probability that I will behave poorly in the future but spares my self-esteem. Like all of us, I do not see myself clearly.

The story of my student did not end with self-deception. She had to come to terms later with what happened. She had to take her behavior out of her "not sex" file and move it to a "sex" file. She had to acknowledge her behavior for what it was. My student's self-esteem does not need to be tied to her sexual behavior in high school anymore. Her self-esteem resides in value that has been given to her by God and cannot be taken away. Confession, forgiveness, and redemption are available to Christians. *Our value is not found in our good behavior or accomplishments but in the identity we have been given by God. Having our self-esteem needs met should allow us look at the world more accurately.* If we can take the self-esteem motive out of the equation by getting self-esteem needs met thought a secure identity in Christ, it will not be competing with the pursuit of accuracy. Maybe we can avoid depression *and* have the courage it takes to love the tainted world and ourselves.

After reading about the origins of bias that are built into our desires to be right and feel good about ourselves, you should have an increased appreciation for the reality of bias, but you may have difficulty

---

[49]Steve Loughnan, Nick Haslam, and Brock Bastian, "The Role of Meat Consumption in the Denial of Moral Status and Mind to Meat Animals," *Appetite* 55, no. 1 (2010): 156-59. "Moral status" was defined by Loughnan et al. (2010) as the ability to experience eighteen different cognitive states (Hassam et al., 2008) combined with responses to two questions: "How much does this cow deserve moral treatment?" and "How unpleasant would it be to harm this cow?" (1 = not at all; 7 = very much so).

[50]David C. Glass, "Changes in Liking as a Means of Reducing Cognitive Discrepancies Between Self-Esteem and Aggression," *Journal of Personality* 32, no. 4 (1964): 531-49, https://doi.org/10.1111/j.1467-6494.1964.tb01357.x.

understanding how bias can be reduced given the entrenched nature of these processes. The manifestation of our desire to be right in the use of schemas and cognitive efficiency hacks combined with our desire to maintain self-esteem create real barriers to accuracy. This writing is my attempt to write a redemption story—to acknowledge the bias, to acknowledge the difficulty inherent in the pursuit of the unbiased, and to propose a roadmap toward becoming less biased. The roadmap begins with our motivations. We want to be right, and we want to feel good about ourselves. If instead of just being motivated to believe we are right, we pursue accuracy by recognizing the incompleteness of our file folders and seeking out disconfirming information, we can be more accurate and less biased. If we can get our self-esteem needs met because our identities are secure in Christ, we can pursue what is righteous without the biasing force of self-esteem maintenance motives. We can be less biased, but as the bias blind spot literature suggests, less cognitive bias won't come from just learning about bias.[51] Instead, you will have to focus your attention on *your own bias.*

CHAPTER ONE SUMMARY

This chapter charts two origins of cognitive bias: the desire to be right, and the desire to maintain self-esteem. Given that we do not have the cognitive capacity to process all incoming stimuli, the process of pursuing what is right begins when schemas (file folders) are created to help collect and organize information. Schemas are *useful* in helping us navigate the world, but bias emerges because schemas are *incomplete* and we don't always recognize their incompleteness. Likewise, schemas are *useful* as filters to guide the processing of new information, but we don't always realize when we *miss or distort* important information because of the filter. Schemas and heuristics are *useful* in helping us think more efficiently but may involve an *accuracy*

---

[51]West, Meserve, and Stanovich, "Cognitive Sophistication Does Not Attenuate the Bias Blind Spot."

trade-off. These basic cognitive processes are necessary, but they contribute to bias and are difficult to change. Instead of believing we are right, we need to *pursue accuracy* by seeking out more and disconfirming information. Our motivation to feel good about ourselves is another contributor to bias because people will distort what is true to maintain self-esteem. *If self-esteem needs are met, people are freed up to pursue accuracy. Christians, having a secure identity in Christ with self-esteem needs met, ought to be more accurate.*

APPLICATION: UNBIASED NUDGE

- Consider that you are biased by your own thinking and that the research on bias applies to you.

- Think of a time when your desire to be right has come into conflict with your desire to feel good about yourself.

TWO

WHO YOU THINK YOU ARE CREATES BIAS

IF FILE FOLDERS ARE THE FUNDAMENTAL unit of thinking, then opening the "self" file folder has very important implications, since it is the biggest file folder and it is chronically open. No one has figured out how to keep this file folder closed. If the "self" file folder is chronically open, *the content of the file matters,* for a reason best termed "self-schematicity,"[1] which means that the important pieces of our self-concept will guide how we process new information, including making judgments about other people.[2] A self-schema is in many ways like any other schema discussed in the last chapter, in that the self-schema guides attention and helps us operate efficiently.[3] In a similar way to our creation of other schemas, we want to be right, even, if not especially, in our self-schema, which leads us to filter information to confirm what we already think about the self, rather than view the self objectively or accurately. On the other hand, the self-schema is unique relative to other schemas because of its size and relationship to self-esteem maintenance. The self-schema contains the information that is most important to our own self-concept; the

[1]Hazel Markus, Jeanne Smith, and Richard L. Moreland, "Role of the Self-Concept in the Perception of Others," *Journal of Personality and Social Psychology* 49, no. 6 (1985): 1494-1512.

[2]Hazel Markus, "Self-Schemata and Processing Information About the Self," *Journal of Personality and Social Psychology* 35, no. 2 (1977): 63-78, https://doi.org/10.1037/0022-3514.35.2.63.

[3]A. C. Graesser and G. V. Nakamura, "The Impact of a Schema on Comprehension and Memory," in *Psychology of Learning and Motivation*, vol. 16 (San Diego, CA: Academic Press, 1982), 59-109; Gerd Gigerenzer and Wolfgang Gaissmaier, "Heuristic Decision Making," *Annual Review of Psychology* 62, no. 1 (2011): 451-82.

mind organizes the important information into the big subfolders of the larger identity folder.

Let's begin by tracing the history and development of the self-schema specifically. Most researchers agree that the self-schema begins at around eighteen months. When my children were around six months, they were not yet mobile but could sit independently. In an effort to entertain them, I would place them in front of a large mirror. This was entertaining because I had basically given them a friend. At this stage of development, babies are not yet able to separate the self from the environment; therefore, they possess no self-schema. Human faces are one of the most interesting things to babies, and since I couldn't stare at my babies without taking time to cook or do laundry, a mirror provided a handy form of entertainment. At around eighteen months old, babies start to distinguish their bodies from the environment, and this is measured by a cute demonstration.[45] Imagine putting a baby in front of a mirror and drawing a red mark on the baby's nose with clown makeup. Before eighteen months, the baby is likely to try to touch the other baby in the mirror and might even touch the mirror baby's nose to wipe off the mark. By eighteen months, the baby looks in the mirror, but touches her own nose. This tell us that at this point in development, even though the baby cannot use language to explain the self, the baby knows that the other baby in the mirror is a reflection of the self, not another baby friend. This is when psychologists claim the self-schema begins.

WHO YOU THINK YOU ARE BIASES YOU

This process of self-schema development is motivated by a desire to be right about ourselves, not to become accurate or righteous, but to figure out how to navigate the world. As young children, we are

---

[4]Beulah Amsterdam, "Mirror Self-Image Reactions Before Age Two," *Developmental Psychobiology* 5, no. 4 (1972): 297-305.

[5]Geert Stienissen, "Rouge Test (Self-Recognition Test)," YouTube, March 14, 2011, www.youtube.com/watch?v=M2I0kwSua44.

trying to figure out what makes us unique. A child might adopt the label of "the funny one" because they received laughter in response to their jokes. Another child might endorse the label of "the pretty one" after having gotten compliments on their appearance from others.[6] I told my oldest daughter going into kindergarten that some kids would be better than her at different things. When she came home, she told me that she was "good at reading, but other kids were better at cutting." This type of self-knowledge is gained through social comparison,[7] and these labels become the subfolders of the self-schema. We look at other people and measure our differences. You are the "pretty one" if others are uglier. Likewise, you are the 'funny one" when other people are less funny. Another way we learn about ourselves is through examining our behaviors.[8] I may consider myself to be a workaholic if I count up the number of hours I spend working. People may consider themselves to be fast drivers if they have received more than five speeding tickets this year. Comparing ourselves to others and examining our own behaviors are methods to learn more about the self.

As the self-schema starts to fill, it becomes too unwieldy, just like the "puppy" file folder did for my daughter. So, we start to organize the information within the "self" file folder. Given the constraints of memory, we do not keep all the information, even as it relates to the self. There are things that happen to us that are forgotten.[9] The amount of incoming information that is related to the self is not possible for our minds to process and organize well. Even the self-schema is incomplete.[10] So instead of thinking of the self-schema as containing all

[6]Timothy D. Wilson and Elizabeth W. Dunn, "Self-Knowledge: Its Limits, Value, and Potential for Improvement," *Annual Review of Psychology* 55, no. 1 (2004): 493-518.

[7]Jerry Suls, René Martin, and Ladd Wheeler, "Social Comparison: Why, with Whom, and with What Effect?," *Current Directions in Psychological Science* 11, no. 5 (2002): 159-63.

[8]D. J. Bem, "Self-Perception Theory," in *Advances in Experimental Social Psychology*, vol. 6 (San Diego, CA: Academic Press, 1972), 1-62.

[9]Anthony G. Greenwald, "Self and Memory," *Psychology of Learning and Motivation* 15 (1981): 201-36.

[10]Hazel Markus, "Self-Schemata and Processing Information About the Self," *Journal of Personality and Social Psychology* 35, no. 2 (1977): 63-78.

the things that have ever happened to us, it makes sense to think about two different self-concepts. The *available self-concept* is everything about the self that we have organized and might be able to access if something prods our memories.[11] This is a huge file folder. I often think of the available self-concept as the combination of everything from the hard drives of every computer I have ever owned in one giant file folder. On the other hand, the *working self-concept* is what we are currently activating about the self.[12] Think of the working self-concept as the open files on a computer's desktop. We have a few files and windows that we leave open so we can easily access them the next time we open the computer. In the language of the self, the working self-concept is the aspects of the self that are relevant to our current situation. When voting, we are likely thinking about our national and political identities. When with parents, we think about our identity as a son or daughter. Thus, the working self-concept is not stable because it shifts given differing context, environment, and motivation, while the available self-concept is relatively stable because it is less context dependent.[13]

As we interact in the world, we are guided by the working self-concept, but there are pieces of the available self-concept that might have proved useful had they been developed and reinforced in childhood. The available self-concept develops over the course of childhood and adulthood though the consolidation of memories.[14] The available self-concept loses information through forgetting.[15] The working self-concept develops as a result of daily practices. We

[11]H. Markus and E. Wurf, "The Dynamic Self-Concept: A Social Psychological Perspective," *Annual Review of Psychology* 38, no. 1 (1987): 299-337.

[12]Hazel Markus and Ziva Kunda, "Stability and Malleability of the Self-Concept," *Journal of Personality and Social Psychology* 51, no. 4 (1986): 858-66.

[13]Markus and Kunda, "Stability and Malleability of the Self-Concept."

[14]Timothy J. Ricker, "The Role of Short-Term Consolidation in Memory Persistence," *AIMS Neuroscience* 2, no. 4 (2015): 259-79.

[15]Jefferson A. Singer and Martin A. Conway, "Should We Forget Forgetting?," *Memory Studies* 1, no. 3 (2008): 279-85.

activate aspects of the self that help us navigate the world.[16] Think of your own childhood. Consider the feedback you received from teachers, parents, and peers about what you were like. Perhaps, you were told that you were the "athletic one," the "smart one," the "funny one," or the "pretty one." Did that affect how you navigated life? If you were the funny one growing up, you might have relied on jokes to help get you out of tough situations. Aspects of the self that help you navigate the world, like being the "funny one," are likely to be activated frequently because of their utility. In a more concrete way, if you were the "athletic one," it is likely that this aspect of the self was frequently activated because your parents enrolled you in sports. Frequently activating these aspects of self becomes habitual over time so not only was being the "funny one" or the "athletic one" something that became a regular part of the working self-concept, but you also became self-schematic for it. Had you been placed in different environments and been encouraged for different skills, different aspects of your identity might have become part of your working self-concept.

Participants in an experiment were asked to select adjectives that described themselves from a list that included words such as *independent, honest, intelligent, friendly,* and *ambitious*. The participants were sorted into groups based on whether they selected the word *independent* as self-descriptive. Then participants completed a task in which experimenters measured how quickly participants were able to categorize the words as either describing "me" or "not me." Not surprisingly, participants who had earlier selected *independent* as self-descriptive, were faster at categorizing independent-related words in the "me" category. Subsequent to this study, a body of research emerged to demonstrate that people who are schematic for particular traits are "chronically sensitive" to things that are consistent with the

---

[16]William B. Swann, Christine Chang-Schneider, and Katie Larsen McClarty, "Do People's Self-Views Matter? Self-Concept and Self-Esteem in Everyday Life," *American Psychologist* 62, no. 2 (2007): 84-94.

schema.[17] Chronic sensitivity is another way of saying that there are aspects of the self that are part of the working self-concept most of the time. Rarely do these aspects get moved to the storage room of the available self-concept. They are the files that are always open on our mind's desktop. Those files are who we think we are most of time. To find out what "self" subfolders you have, stop and take a minute to complete this sentence ten times with the first things that come to mind: "I am _____."[18] Whatever answers come to mind first reflect subfolders that are most likely your larger ones because they were the easiest for your mind to access. This information comes directly from the working self-concept that is open frequently on the desktop of your mind. You might have filled in the blank with trait words, as most Americans do, such as *smart, interesting, funny, hardworking,* or *patient.*[19] You might have included some group membership words, such as *daughter, mother, social worker, caregiver,* or *church member.* A third category of subfolders are behavior terms: a person who *studies, plays baseball, makes omelets,* or *does laundry.* The final category of subfolders, one that most people don't think of, contain universal descriptors such as *human,* a *child of God,* or a *sinner saved by grace.*

The information in the "self" file folder is far from neutral. Whatever is chronically accessible takes your time and attention and affects your performance. Researchers compared the performance of equally academically capable students who self-identified as "problem solvers" to those who did not identify that way, on a series of logical reasoning

[17]Susan E. Cross and Hazel Rose Markus, "Self-Schemas, Possible Selves, and Competent Performance," *Journal of Educational Psychology* 86, no. 3 (1994): 423-38, https://doi.org/10.1037/0022 0663.86.3.423.

[18]Manford H. Kuhn and Thomas S. McPartland, "Twenty Statements Test," PsycTESTS Dataset, 1954; Raymond Montemayor and Marvin Eisen, "The Development of Self-Conceptions from Childhood to Adolescence," *Developmental Psychology* 13, no. 4 (1977): 314-19.

[19]Chad Gordon, "Self-Conceptions; Configurations of Content" in *The Self in Social Interaction,* vol. 1: *Classic and Contemporary Perspectives,* ed. Chad Gordon and Kenneth J. Gergen (New York: J. Wiley, 1968), 115-36.

tasks. Halfway through the reasoning tasks, half of the participants were told that they performed at the 47th percentile (failure feedback) or received no feedback. Students who thought of themselves as "problem solvers" tried their best on the tasks no matter what they were told by the experimenters. The participants who did not think of themselves as "problem solvers" only tried hard when they were threatened with failure.[20] Let me translate: when something like "problem solving" is important to a person's self-concept, people try hard. People who think of themselves as problem solvers will try to problem-solve regardless of the perceived value of the particular task. The implication of this research is that we need to be aware and strategic in how we organize the self-schema because we will give our best effort toward things that are important to the self-concept. The development of the self-concept was and is an attempt to create an accurate view of the self, but it is based on other people's perceptions of us and our assessments of our behaviors. Aspects of the self that don't get regularly activated fade in memory and utility, but under different conditions might have been nurtured. Who we think we are not only impacts what we spend time thinking about, but it also impacts how we judge others.[21]

WHO YOU THINK YOU ARE BIASES YOUR VIEW OF OTHERS

I don't have a large subfolder of my "self" file labeled "athleticism." I was not the "athletic one" growing up, and I don't pretend to be an athlete now. My husband was a gymnast and did the rings in college. Even now as an adult, he keeps a regular gym routine that I could not pretend to do or understand. His frequent gym attendance and large subfolder for athleticism means that he has other friends who share his love of fitness. I distinctly recall one day when we were at a mall,

---

[20]Cross and Markus, "Self-Schemas, Possible Selves, and Competent Performance."
[21]Geoffrey T. Fong and Hazel Markus, "Self-Schemas and Judgments About Others," *Social Cognition* 1, no. 3 (1982): 191-204.

and he said, "Hey, is that Stewart walking ahead of us?" This person was a good hundred yards ahead of us and we were looking at his back. I said, "Why do you think that?" To which my husband replied, "I think I recognize his lats." This response earned him a wide-eyed repetition from me: "His lats? What are lats?!" Turns out it was Stewart. Not having a large subfolder for athleticism means there are whole features of people I don't see because I have no folder for lats—strong ones or otherwise. Having a large subfolder for athleticism means that my husband can and does size up Mark Wahlberg's athleticism on a whole slew of features that I don't code.

That example might sound innocuous. Maybe judging other people's athleticism doesn't really matter, but this self-schematic effect will emerge on any trait that matters to your sense of self.[22] You are *judgmental* on the categories that matter to your self-schema. For example, women especially feel judged based on their attractiveness and can easily answer whether they were the "pretty one" growing up. I realize that I am stating something so obvious it barely warrants typing on a page. Women have a self-assessment of their own attractiveness, and the more this idea is central to the sense of self, the more it also gets used to judge others.[23] For example, I was standing in line to ride roller coasters at an amusement park in the Midwest one summer, and I overheard the conversation of the woman in front of me in line. She was judging which other women in the line should not have been scantily dressed. This woman herself was severely below a normal body weight, in a way that made me think she was suffering from anorexia. Hearing the woman make these comments about other women's bodies made it very hard for me to not comment that there might also be something wrong with how she was starving her

[22]Mark W. Baldwin, "Relational Schemas and the Processing of Social Information," *Psychological Bulletin* 112, no. 3 (1992): 461-84.

[23]Hazel Markus, Ruth Hamill, and Keith P. Sentis, "Thinking Fat: Self-Schemas for Body Weight and the Processing of Weight Relevant Information 1," *Journal of Applied Social Psychology* 17, no. 1 (1987): 50-71.

own body. Now, years later, I realize that it is likely that this woman was constantly thinking about weight and body fat for herself, which made it nearly impossible that she wouldn't apply those same ideas to the people around her. She probably had no idea that I was appalled by her comments.

I was particularly struck by the judgmental way that we use "self" subfolders to guide our attention when I attended the graduation ceremony at a well-regarded university. As is typical, a representative of the university's alumni association came to speak to the graduates, inviting them to connect with the alumni association, which is an implicit request to give money. The woman gave a rousing speech stating in effect, "When things get hard, when you want to give up, keep going by reminding yourself that you are a graduate of _____ University." That line became the refrain of her speech, reminding yourself that "You are a graduate of _____ University." My girls and I looked at each other and laughed. If you are being chased by a bear, be sure to tell it that "You are a graduate of _____ University." Even they realized that this does not offer much consolation when life is hard.

So why did the woman giving the speech think it made sense? Why didn't anyone in the audience laugh at the ridiculous idea that an affiliation with a prestigious university would be the inspiration a person needs to keep going? We want to believe that prestige alone is enough to add value to a person's life. Whenever we are in a conversation and someone casually name drops or offhandedly mentions a prestigious affiliation, it is a way of subtly communicating worth or value. Like all potential placebos, if you can believe it, it might work.[24] What I mean is, if you truly believe that getting a degree from a prestigious university is a sign that you are a superior person who is more capable than others, this might be the extra motivation you need to

---

[24]Gunver S. Kienle and Helmut Kiene, "The Powerful Placebo Effect: Fact or Fiction?," *Journal of Clinical Epidemiology* 50, no. 12 (1997): 1311–18.

keep going. In that sense, the alumni representative is right. The very unfortunate side effect of regularly activating the "prestige" file folder is that we judge other people as less valuable when they don't have the same level of prestige as we do.

God's assessments of us are not focused on athleticism, attractiveness, or prestige. This could be said of a million other traits that can be used to guide my attention on myself and others. I used to think of myself as "independent," and this was central to my "self" file folder. Turns out no one is as independent as I thought I was, including myself, and using that to find similarity and friendship wasn't very useful. I have also been accused of making people feel like they have to be over-the-top interesting. My judgmentalism on certain traits like "independent" and "interesting" are subfolders that I want to change. I have a subfolder for "interesting," but I don't want to be such a snob about judging how "interesting" or "fun" people are. So how does a person become less judgmental? By changing what is in the "self" file folder. What is in my "self" file folder is different than what *should be* in the "self" file folder. I had to think hard about what was true and important about humans generally, and about myself. What is or should be part of a deeper and more accurate identity? If I were to think about my self-schema in terms of the first of the four categories described earlier (traits), I have tried to cultivate valuable traits like honesty, but trait-wise we are all flawed. If I think about my self in terms of group identities, it is not my relational titles that are my source of value. Behaviors like accomplishments are small comfort in the face of tragedy or the size of the world's problems. I value accomplishments, but they aren't what make me valuable. Traits, group memberships, and behaviors are not the sum total of who we are. All of these are subject to failures and successes, but for Christians, the value of the self is constant.

What is left if you strip the traits and titles? I am a child of God and a sinner saved by grace. I have a position of worth that cannot be taken away, and I am not perfect. This leads to the thesis of this book, that *identity as a child of God and a sinner saved by grace ought to provide stability to self-esteem* (Galatians 3:26; Ephesians 2:8-9). *This is our most accurate identity; therefore, this is what should be the most accessible part of our "self" file folder.* We are most accurate when this is the part of our identity that is chronically activated. When we think about ourselves as a child of God, we have nothing to prove. We don't need to sell our value to others. Recognizing our shared position as sinners reminds us to be humble and to acknowledge the fallibility of our thinking. This identity as children of God and sinners saved by grace resolves the need to feel good as a motivation that influences how we file information in our file folders. With our motivation to maintain self-esteem satisfied, we can pursue accuracy and right-eousness. If we don't have to boost self-esteem by only accessing the file folders designed to maintain it, we ought to be more accepting of failure. We ought to be more willing to be wrong, to take risks, to apologize, to change behavior instead of attitudes, to forgive others, to be generous, to avoid stereotypes, to think slowly when forming impressions, to be slow in forming opinions, to be willing to revise opinions in light of new evidence, and to embrace ambivalence. The more I open this "child of God" file folder, the less judgmental and more similar I feel to all the other humans around me, the more honest I am with myself, and the more peaceful I feel about the possibility of failure and loss.

WHO YOU THINK YOU ARE CREATES YOUR CONTEXT FOR FAILURE

After reading the previous section, I hope you are inspired by the idea that once we shift our identities to be children of God and sinners saved by grace, we are freed up to pursue accuracy and to fail in other areas of our lives because our self-esteem is not rooted in our perfor-mance. This is an easy sentence for me to write because it makes so much sense to me. Unfortunately, living out this idea is hard. The idea of shifting our identities to ones at which we cannot fail emerged for me out of self-complexity theory.[25] Self-complexity theory is an idea that you are buffered from the negative effects of failure if you have multiple ways of thinking about yourself. If I consider that I am a mom, a wife, a professor, a daughter, and so on, failing in one of those areas will be less damaging because I have other roles to fall back on. Losing my professional job will hurt less as long as my identity is spread out into these other roles. At least, I can think of myself as a good mom if I can no longer consider myself to be a good professor. This theory, which does have some empirical support, suggests that failure is a threat to self-esteem in situations where failure is a possibility.[26] *Thus, in most cases, identities are subject to the possibility of failure.* Where we place our identity becomes our context for failure. I could lose my job, get divorced, become alienated from my family, or lose my health. If self-esteem is tied to these roles, my self-esteem is vulnerable because failure is possible. The "buffering" hypothesis of multiple identities and roles makes sense for categories at which you can fail. Being a child of God and sinner saved by grace is not an identity at which any human can fail. I try to remind myself that this is my primary identity and I try not to build too much self-esteem based on my other subfolder identities. This is much more difficult than it sounds.

I was confronted with this difficulty when my youngest daughter's first day of kindergarten coincided with my fifteen-year wedding anniversary. I spent a lot of time with my girls during their preschool years. That said, I have always been a working mom. In addition to my professor job and my mom job, I have been doing consulting work on the side for the past five years. Based on self-complexity theory,

---

[25]Patricia W. Linville, "Self-Complexity and Affective Extremity: Don't Put All of Your Eggs in One Cognitive Basket," *Social Cognition* 3, no. 1 (1985): 94-120.
[26]Eshkol Rafaeli-Mor and Jennifer Steinberg, "Self-Complexity and Well-Being: A Review and Research Synthesis," *Personality and Social Psychology Review* 6, no. 1 (2002): 31-58.

this shift in my mom identity should be buffered by these other identities, not to mention my argument that as a child of God and sinner saved by grace, I shouldn't be placing too much value in these other identities anyway. For these reasons, one might predict that I would drop off my daughters at school, come home, and have a great time celebrating my anniversary, writing this book, and enjoying the quiet that allows me to pursue my other identities uninterrupted. This is not what happened.

I could barely sleep the night before. I had a raging headache that only got worse after the hours of crying that happened after I dropped my youngest daughter off. I had taken a video of her wearing her giant backpack and waving to me as she walked into school for the first time that I watched on and off all day. Even after taking ibuprofen, the headache was too strong for me to concentrate on anything work-related, and I didn't feel like celebrating. In response to my strong emotional reaction, my husband was not sure how to react or provide comfort in response to what he perceived as an overreaction. In both the mom subfolder and the wife subfolder, I was experiencing some significant discomfort.

I gave myself a bit of time to be sad about the girls having graduated from the preschool era. Then I gave myself a bit of emotional distance to look at the origin of this response. My wife and mother identities are identities that feel too big to fail. I did not even fail in these two categories, but their disruption was enough to lead to a strong physical response. I had trouble eating, sleeping, not crying, and avoiding headaches. I do not know if it is possible for me to avoid placing value on my success in these identities. It makes sense to me cognitively that my value is not in those identities, but emotionally, a feeling of calmness when those identities are shaken feels unattainable. Given this contradiction, I am led to question whether it is good advice to avoid basing self-esteem on success in these categories. Or, just because I am failing to do something that does not mean that it is not worth pursuing. When I was trying to process the grief I felt dropping my daughter off, I was comforted to think of my identity as a child of God and sinner saved by grace. It did not end the headache, but it helped me reorient as I learned to adjust. It is inevitable that my "mom" file folder is going to take more hits, and for the foreseeable future, my automatic response is likely to be strong and emotional. I can imagine years from now that maybe I will have learned to accept changes and failures in my "mom" and "wife" file folders with greater emotional stability.

There is a video of Bible teacher and mega-author Beth Moore discussing her greatest fears, one of which is that her husband falls in love with a woman half her age, her children love the new woman, and her grandchildren call her something like "Mimi or Fifi."[27] She says that if her husband left her, it would be much better if her daughters and grandchildren hated his new wife. After describing her nightmare scenario, she asks the audience to answer the question, "Then what?" The answer to that question is stuff like crying, anger, having to attend a baby's birth with Fifi, and devastation. Beth asks again, "Then what?" At the end of the day, she says, she would "get on the floor, have a fit, cry her eyes out, and then bury her face in the Scriptures, cry out to God to redeem her pain, and work it through until it bears fruit that never passes away." Eventually, she says, "By God's grace I am going to get up." This feels more emotionally right to me than never emotionally responding when the identity subfolders are shaken. We are humans who have been blessed with identities that we care about, but they shouldn't consume us completely. The answer to the "Then what?" question when those identities are shaken is, "We are still God's children and sinners saved by grace." *We are going to trust God and get back up again even after we fail in the identities that feel too big to fail.* Our deepest and most accurate identity is secure.

---

[27]Jacques Jean, "If and Then | Part 3 | Beth Moore | Christian Videos," YouTube, December 28, 2018, www.youtube.com/watch?v=Og_4ZfWYcH4.

YOU ARE A SINNER SAVED BY GRACE

When we experience failure in major sources of identity, it is helpful to remember that we are sharing in a common experience of humanity. We are all born, we will all fail at things, and we will all die. The feeling that no one else can understand our pain, and no one has ever failed in the same way we have, is isolating.[28] This is one of the reasons that *thinking of yourself as a sinner saved by grace should have power to reduce negative feelings.* You are no longer alone in your screw-ups when you recognize that we are all sinners—that no one is holy, not even one of us. The "sinner saved by grace" subfolder offers us a way to normalize our experience and practice self-compassion.

Imagine, as social psychologist E. Tory Higgins argues, that you have three selves: an ideal self, an ought self, and an actual self.[29] The ideal self is the person you hope to be. This person might be a famous singer, own a beach house, and love everyone unconditionally. Take a moment and think about who your ideal self is. The ought self is who you think you should be. This person might be honest, loyal, forgiving, and unbiased. Take a minute and think about who your ought self is. The actual self is the one you are. Now consider how your actual self is different from your ideal self and different from your ought self. The bigger those differences are, the more negative feelings you might be experiencing. According to self-discrepancy theory, we feel depressed when our ideal selves are too different from our actual selves, and we feel anxious when our ought selves are too different from our actual selves.[30] To drive this point home in class, I set a timer for one minute and have students think about the ideal self-actual self-discrepancy; specifically, the idea that they will never meet any

[28]Nicholas V. Karayannis et al., "The Impact of Social Isolation on Pain Interference: A Longitudinal Study," *Annals of Behavioral Medicine* 53, no. 1 (2018): 65-74.

[29]E. Tory Higgins, "Self-Discrepancy: A Theory Relating Self and Affect," *Psychological Review* 94, no. 3 (1987): 319-40.

[30]E. Tory Higgins, "Self-Discrepancy Theory: What Patterns of Self-Beliefs Cause People to Suffer?," in *Advances in Experimental Social Psychology*, vol. 22 (San Diego, CA: Academic Press, 1989), 93-136.

of the qualifications of the ideal self. I set the stage by explaining my own. My ideal self is an inspiring Christian example, married, good mother, and a professor that helps students. To imagine the discrepancy, I imagine that on my deathbed, I am alone because my kids hate me, my husband divorced me years ago, and I was of no use to any of my former students. Hopefully, spending a minute thinking about a discrepancy like that helps you understand why a discrepancy between your ideal self and actual self is depressing.

When I discuss self-discrepancy theory in class, I have a less-than-flattering picture of E. Tory Higgins that I put on the screen. I don't think the picture represents his ideal self (although I really have no idea). Then I ask students to imagine if a friend were to post a less-than-flattering picture of them on social media. This might feel like a discrepancy between the ideal self and actual self, so you might feel depressed that you don't look the way you wish you did. If a friend posts a picture of you on social media that shows you violating a standard, either a moral or hygienic standard, you might feel anxious that you will lose relationships with people because you have done something that reveals that your actual self is not consistent with your ought self.

As part of my job, I have students that are my designated advisees, whom I guide through the psychology program during the three-to-five years they are enrolled. I remember sitting down with a student early in my career, discussing that she was still a few courses short of a spring graduation. I remember her pleading with me, thinking that she could convince me to let her walk at graduation even though she had not completed the required coursework. Looking back, I am a bit astonished that she thought I was that powerful. Regardless, as she continued to plead with me, it became clear that her entire family thought she was graduating that spring. They had bought plane tickets, made hotel reservations, and were excited to watch their oldest child receive a degree. Their ideal daughter and their ought daughter were graduating from college, but their actual daughter was not. In addition to our own ideal and ought self, important people in our lives have their own ideal and ought versions of us. When we don't live up to their ideal versions of us, we are depressed. When we don't live up to their ought versions of us, we are ashamed and scared they will abandon us. It took me a while to convince the student that she needed to call her parents to explain the situation.

In the same way we feel upset when we fail in parts of our identity that are meaningful to us, discrepancies between our actual, ideal, and ought selves are signals either that we have failed or have not yet achieved the ideal or ought version of ourselves. When I gave the maid-of-honor speech at a dear friend's wedding, I talked about how I was confident that the bride and groom would be good partners not because they were perfect people, but because they had shared ideal selves and partners. Imagine you are sitting down to counsel a couple who is engaged. You ask each of them to separately describe what their ideal marriage partner would be like (not the actual partner that they came with). Next, you ask them to describe who they themselves would ideally want to be at the end of their lives. If each partner's ideal spouse is their partner's ideal self, this is a good match. Everyone will fail to live up to ideals, but I am in a much better position to forgive my partner if I think he is trying to be the partner I want him to be. If he forgets to take out the trash, I will forgive him because I know he really wants to be a helpful spouse. Likewise, I am much more likely to apologize when I fail to be the person my partner wants me to be because that is also the person that I want to be. I am sorry when I forget to pick up something from the store because I want to be a helpful spouse. Marriage is easier when people are quick to apologize and forgive, and this is more likely when ideal spouses and ideal selves match.

I started giving the "ideal self, ideal partner" match advice when my husband and I lived on a Catholic college campus, in response to questions about whether it was a good idea to date someone who was not Catholic. In evangelical circles, when someone asks if whether it's okay to date a non-Christian, the easy answer is "Do not be yoked together with unbelievers" (2 Corinthians 6:14). This answer feels a bit too pat to someone who isn't part of a subculture that references oxen, so I realized that it makes more sense to frame it as a difference in ideal selves. A person's ought and ideal selves are shaped by faith. Who I want to be and who I should be are informed largely by ideas like the "fruits of the spirit" (Galatians 5:22) or the 1 Corinthians 13 love chapter. These are held in common for most Christians. We are equally yoked when we are pursuing the same ideal selves. A Christian dating someone who is not even trying to be holy will be facing an uphill battle to convince them to be. One or both partners will become a nag. If partners share ideals, the nagging should not be necessary, or at least will be less frequent.

This sharing of ideal selves is not restricted to married couples. We ought to "spur one another on toward love and good deeds" (Hebrews 10:24). This is encouragement to live up to our ideal selves. In the same way married couples should be more forgiving when their partners fail because they know they are trying to live up to their ideals, we should be more forgiving of others and ourselves, especially in the faith, when they fail. We are all sinners saved by grace.

In order to test the idea that thinking about an identity as a sinner saved by grace ought to increase perceptions of discrepancy, but ultimately reduce negative feelings attached to the discrepancy, I conducted an experiment with my students.[31] Some students were instructed to fill an entire page describing the nature of God, and some were instructed to write about their plans for the day. Both groups completed Higgins's self-discrepancy measure, and then a measure of positive and negative emotions. The results confirmed

---

[31] E. E. Devers, A. Mertz, and J. Dudley, "The Effect of God Priming on Self-Discrepancy" (poster, Association for Psychological Science 29th Annual Convention, Boston, May 2017).

that thinking about God increased both ought and ideal discrepancies. Thinking about God makes it more obvious that we aren't measuring up. Perhaps more interestingly, participants who wrote about the nature of God also felt better. They felt more confident and joyful than people who wrote about their plans for the day *even though they had larger self-discrepancies.*

We will fall short of our ideal selves, which is depressing. Paul instructs us to not think of yourself "more highly than you ought, but rather think of yourself with sober judgment, in accordance with the faith God has distributed to each of you" (Romans 12:3). Paul words remind us that thinking about ourselves less highly is depressing, but faith makes it possible for us to do it. We will all fall short of our ought selves. The ideal and ought selves are not our most accurate selves. Our truest identity as sinners saved by grace is secure in the face of failure. Let's remind each other of God's forgiveness. When I fail or witness someone else's failure, *my identity as a sinner saved by grace ought to remind me that failure is part of the human experience*; God, "who began a good work in you," will be faithful to "carry it on to completion until the day of Christ Jesus" (Philippians 1:6), and there is encouragement and forgiveness on offer.

YOU ARE A CHILD OF GOD

Increasingly in our culture success is measured by profit. As a quantitative researcher, I love using numbers to measure things. It feels so much more objective; however, what is objective and easy to measure might not be a valid measure. Validity is about whether the measure is measuring the right thing, and in the case of success, profit is not the best measure of success. If, as is being argued here, identity can be found in being a child of God and a sinner saved by grace or another identity at which you cannot fail, it's an excellent way to prevent threats to self-esteem from clouding an accurate assessment of situations and facts. But finding identity as children of God and sinners saved by grace does not provide a clear roadmap for life decisions because it is a lot fuzzier of a concept than profit.

Measuring success based on money makes choosing a major, choosing a job, and deciding how to allocate time much easier. If money is the goal, pick the major with the most lucrative job prospects, choose the job with the biggest financial rewards, and spend time on things that will earn you more money including side hustles. If success in life is measured based on enjoyment, choosing a job in a location that offers more leisure possibilities, like beaches, restaurants, and so on, is important. If the goal is to make the most of time with family, choosing a job with a flexible schedule in a location with good schools and a reasonable cost of living is the sensible corresponding strategy. If success is not measured in any of those dimensions, if success has already been secured just based on an identity that can't be taken away, the possibilities are so large as to render decisions difficult.

The decision-making component of a worldview is important. Terror management theory, despite its frightening name, is one of my favorite theories because it asserts that self-esteem is based on having a consistent worldview and believing that you are living in a way that is consistent with that worldview.[32] This makes so much sense as you consider the thoughts of a person facing death. While thinking about death is unpleasant, it is more pleasant for people who believe they understand what the purpose of life is and have lived lives consistent with that purpose. A secure self-identity ought to be consistent with what a person considers to be life's purpose.

I propose that there needs to be a worldview and decision-making framework related to what it means to be children of God. The "child of God" file folder should regularly activate and be useful; thus, it needs to be connected to daily decision-making. I will try to explain

---

[32]Tom Pyszczynski, Sheldon Solomon, and Jeff Greenberg, "Thirty Years of Terror Management Theory: From Genesis to Revelation," in *Advances in Experimental Social Psychology*, vol. 52 (San Diego, CA: Academic Press, 2015), 1-70.

by imperfectly extending the analogy of the "child of God" subfolder to my own children. I adore them. I love watching what they do, celebrating their joy, delighting in their learning, and cuddling them under blankets. In addition to just enjoying their presence, I am also trying to help them grow, participate in our home, and prepare for their eventual lives as adults. They are asked to participate in the work of the home by doing small chores, but the responsibility for the home is not theirs to hold. Whether the bank might repossess the house, or the house might collapse because of structural damage is not something that my kids consider, but they are helpful with laundry. As a parent, I can only imagine that God delights in us as I delight in my kids. I can also imagine that God is inviting us to participate in improving the world, but not to assume the responsibility for achieving ultimate justice on earth. If this is what it means to be children of God, it is characterized by love and service. We should be giving and receiving love from God and serving others.

In terms of decision-making, loving and serving ought to be top of mind, not because they are measures of success but because they are *outcomes of an identity* as children of God. Developing and living in an identity as children of God means participating in spiritual disciplines. If God is my father, then I am going to talk to God, rely on God, ask God how I can help around the house, or around the world. I'm going to put myself in a position to love and be loved by God by spending time with him and the people that he loves. To continue the analogy, a good day in the life of my children ought to include spending time with mom and dad, helping around the house, playing with each other, practicing kindness, and learning something that will be useful. It seems like this would be a good day as a child of God as well. We should be spending time with God, serving people, enjoying something, practicing kindness, and learning something useful.

Love and service as guiding principles still sound very abstract. In practical terms, if love and service are priorities, there ought to be some flexible time to answer God's call, and there ought to be time devoted to spending time with God. Other than that, a life of love and service could look very different for different people. On the one hand, that difference makes giving advice more difficult, but on the other hand, it prevents us from being too judgmental of other people's decisions since a life of love and service can take so many forms. I've caught myself being judgmental of another mom's decision, but the reality is that moms can live a life of love and service that can look very different from each other. I shouldn't measure the love and service of another person, and since I wouldn't be good at measuring it anyway, it's best to assume they are doing it well regardless of how I see it.

If self-identity is primarily rooted in identities at which we could not fail, we can have a more accurate and consistent worldview, believe we are living in ways that are consistent with the worldview, and be less judgmental of others. *If we begin to live from a more accurate identity, it becomes easier to build a worldview and decision-making framework that is more accurate and righteous. We can be less biased.* After reading this chapter, you should feel better prepared to live in a way that is less biased because you have changed your self-concept to be less biased. Changing the self-concept has the benefit of helping get your self-esteem needs met through a secure identity. Unfortunately, the motive to maintain self-esteem is powerful and can still prevent us from being unbiased, which we will discuss in detail in the next chapter.

CHAPTER TWO SUMMARY

The content of the "self" file folder matters because it biases our judgments of ourselves and others. What we believe is important about ourselves will also provide the context for our failures. We think we are right when we build identities around our traits, group identities, and behaviors. If we had an accurate identity as children of God and sinners saved by grace, we would be more accurate and less judgmental in in our assessments of others. Most of our other identities are subject to the possibility of failure, so in the face of failures, our identities as children of God and sinners saved by grace can provide a buffer. We "do not grieve like the rest of mankind, who have no hope" (1 Thessalonians 4:12-14). We mourn when we fail, but we are buffered by our accurate identity in Christ. Thinking about our identity as sinners saved by grace reminds us that failure is part of being human. Thinking about our identity as children of God reminds us that we are loved in a way that is not contingent on performance. If we were able to build a more accurate identity, worldview, and decision-making framework that centered on being children of God and sinners saved by grace, we would be best positioned to further pursue accuracy because we would be best able to avoid the self-serving biases that will be the focus of chapter three.

APPLICATION: UNBIASED NUDGES

- Consider the way you filled in the blank for "I am _____." Think about what dimensions of the self really matter, and to what degree you want to judge others on those dimensions. Think about yourself as a child of God every day.

- Use your "child of God" and "sinner saved by grace" subfolder to comfort you when your "too big to fail" identity subfolders are rocked by failure.

- Consider the differences between your ideal self, your ought self, and your actual self. Remind yourself that those discrepancies are opportunities for growth, God is not done with you yet, and failure is part of the human experience. You are a "sinner saved by grace."

- At the end of the day, ask yourself if your day was characterized by love and service. Don't do this to pat yourself on the back for being the best. Your value is not based on performance, but you should ask yourself that question to make sure that you are living in a way that is consistent with your identity.

THREE

WHAT YOU BELIEVE ABOUT YOURSELF CREATES BIAS

At this point, you are on your way to a less-biased self through understanding that bias comes from wanting to be right and wanting to feel good about yourself. Additionally, we have discussed how to correct a view of the self that was focused more on traits, group identities, and behaviors than it should have been by instead focusing more attention on the accurate identity we all share as children of God and sinners saved by grace. The original view of the self was created in response to feedback and wanting to be right in our self-assessments. If wanting to be right were the only motivation at play, pursuing accuracy by adjusting the focus of the self away from traits, group identities, and behaviors would be enough to dramatically reduce bias. However, one of the largest sources of bias is the desire to maintain self-esteem.[1] This bias is so strong that it undermines even the sincerest attempts at accuracy. The strong desire to maintain self-esteem is a way of taking all information related to the self, even negative information, and adding a positive spin to it. It's like adding a smiley face emoji after every sentence or adding a dash of salt to every bite of food. No, the mind is not trying to gaslight us, but it is instead trying to portray the best version of the event, not exactly lying, but perhaps exaggerating the truth. My student from the first chapter,

[1]Hua Zhang et al., "Self-Esteem Modulates the Time Course of Self-Positivity Bias in Explicit Self-Evaluation," *PLoS ONE* 8, no. 12 (2013): e81169.

who recategorized her sexual behavior, faced the challenge of maintaining her self-esteem when she was doing something that went against her deeply held beliefs. Her mind protected her self-esteem by initially categorizing her behavior as "not sex." Like my student, *we filter the information we receive through a self-bias*.[2] The self-bias may lead us to sacrifice accuracy to maintain high self-esteem.

There is a funny finding in social psychology research that shows that there are more Charlottes in Charlotte than one would predict based on a normal distribution of names, or more Phils in Philadelphia.[3] Even more surprising is that these Charlottes and Phils were not all born in those places; they are actually more likely to move to them. When asked, it seems very unlikely that Charlotte would say that she moved to Charlotte simply because the city shares her name. Instead, the argument here is that the name-location effect is implicit. People hold a positive self-bias and this bias encompasses their own name, which, in turn, makes favoring all things name-related more likely.[4] A unique auditory response psychologists have termed the "cocktail party effect" explains the way the sound of one's own name from across a crowded room can interrupt even the most fascinating conversation.[5] This self-bias sounds cute in the context I have presented so far, but without a doubt it might lead to a lot more problematic processing if all information is designed to boost self-esteem.

Let's consider another scenario that does not involve moving to a town with name similarities. Imagine you are in an experiment where you are going to receive either failure or success feedback. In one

---

[2]Jie Sui and Glyn W. Humphreys, "The Ubiquitous Self: What the Properties of Self-Bias Tell Us About the Self," *Annals of the New York Academy of Sciences* 1396, no. 1 (2016): 222-35.

[3]Brett W. Pelham, Matthew C. Mirenberg, and John T. Jones, "Why Susie Sells Seashells by the Seashore: Implicit Egotism and Major Life Decisions," *Journal of Personality and Social Psychology* 82, no. 4 (2002): 469-87.

[4]Eric C. Fields and Gina R. Kuperberg, "Loving Yourself More Than Your Neighbor: ERPs Reveal Online Effects of a Self-Positivity Bias," *Social Cognitive and Affective Neuroscience* 10, no. 9 (2015): 1202-9.

[5]Barry Arons, "A Review of the Cocktail Party Effect," *Journal of the American Voice I/O society* 12, no. 7 (1992): 35-50.

version of the experiment, participants were introduced to two couples and then asked to guess which of the two couples were engaged.[6] After guessing, participants were either told they were correct or were incorrect about which couple was engaged. Participants were presented with this task three times and were either given "correct" or "incorrect" for all three of the questions. After completing the three questions, participants took a short break and were told to think about one of their favorite couples. At the conclusion of the break, all participants were asked to identify which three couples of the six were engaged. The question experimenters were asking was whether the participants who got failure feedback remembered more than the participants who got success feedback. In this, and many other experiments like this, the answer is that the participants who were told that they gave the "correct" answer did better remembering the answers than the participants who were told that they gave the 'incorrect" answer, even though amount of information they received was identical.

It turns out that we might not learn as much from failure as popular culture leads us to believe. The reason for this difference in learning is that failure feedback, even on something as inconsequential as the ability to guess which couples are engaged, threatens our self-esteem. When experimenters had participants watch someone else receive the same "failure" feedback, they learned just as much as the participants in the "success" condition.[7] So while it might be a cute finding that the self-bias might lead to favoring things related to the self, it also gets in the way of our ability to learn from our mistakes, which can have far more consequential results. If self-esteem is not on the line, time can be spent on accurately incorporating feedback, which leads to growth, but when self-esteem is

---

[6]Lauren Eskreis-Winkler and Ayelet Fishbach, "Not Learning from Failure—the Greatest Failure of All," *Psychological Science* 30, no. 12 (2019): 1733-44.
[7]Eskreis-Winkler and Fishbach, "Not Learning from Failure—the Greatest Failure of All."

threatened by failure, time must be spent on regulating emotions not accurately assessing the feedback.[8]

In order to avoid the biasing effects of maintaining self-esteem, I will identify three patterns of biased thinking that we employ to maintain self-esteem. We believe that we have more control than we do, we believe that we are more moral than we are, and we wrongly believe we are better than others in an effort to maintain self-esteem. Our self-bias bends incoming information to fit these narratives. Recognizing these faulty beliefs in ourselves takes courage. We need to be honest in how these faulty beliefs serve our self-esteem needs and then relinquish them. We need to get our self-esteem needs met in a secure identity instead. First, we need to look our biased selves in the mirror.

BELIEVING WE ARE IN CONTROL HELPS
US FEEL GOOD ABOUT OURSELVES

It feels good to believe we have control, so we try to file information to maintain that belief even when it is not true.[9] I used to believe I had more control over just about everything in my life, which is funny because as a child I had very little control—I just was not aware of it. In my early twenties, I probably was at my peak sense of control, where I believed implicitly in a just world: that good things happen to good people (or at least to the people who were trying the hardest) and bad things happen to bad people (or at least the laziest people).[10] I thought I could choose my career, pick my spouse, and generally make the right decisions that would lead to a happy life.

Even outside of major life decisions, we like to believe that we have control, which is why we are voyeuristically fascinated with other

---

[8]Felix Grundmann, Susanne Scheibe, and Kai Epstude, "When Ignoring Negative Feedback Is Functional: Presenting a Model of Motivated Feedback Disengagement," *Current Directions in Psychological Science* 30, no. 1 (2020): 3-10.

[9]H. M. Lefcourt, "Belief in Personal Control: Research and Implications," *Journal of Individual Psychology* 22, no. 2 (1966): 185.

[10]Melvin J. Lerner, "The Belief in a Just World," in *The Belief in a Just World: A Fundamental Decision* (Boston: Springer, 1980), 9-30.

people's tragedies. I am sure you have been stuck in traffic on a major highway only to find out that the slowing was not because the accident had blocked traffic, but because the other drivers wanted to stare at the accident. Similarly, I do not think I am alone in a fascination with watching true crime or listening to true crime podcasts. I know that the content will not be a mood booster, and it seems possible that these shows would trigger existential anxiety. Instead, these shows hold the power to reduce anxiety by providing the sense that we have figured out how to prevent bad things from happening to us. On true crime shows, it becomes easy to argue that bad things happen to bad people, or that there are bad situations that can be avoided, so that bad things will not happen. We like to ask people questions about what caused their car accident, divorce, or disease because it makes us feel as though we can control whether those things will happen to us. The belief in a just world protects us from feelings of existential threat, and analyzing another person's tragedy gives us a similarly false belief that we can prevent bad things from happening to us.[11]

Believing we have control helps protect us from living in fear of bad things happening, and it also reflects a portion of reality that helps us succeed. In many ways, in our small everyday actions, we have primary control in setting up our environments and making decisions.[12] Growth mindset is the idea that success in any domain is primarily achieved through effort and not ability.[13] We are more likely to learn statistics, or anything else for that matter, when we believe that it is effort and not simply ability that is required.[14] Believing that we have control over our surroundings is correlated with positive emotions, so

---

[11]Lerner, "The Belief in a Just World."

[12]Jutta Heckhausen and Richard Schulz, "A Life-Span Theory of Control," *Psychological Review* 102, no. 2 (1995): 284-304.

[13]Carol S. Dweck, *Mindset: The New Psychology of Success* (New York: Random House, 2006), 7.

[14]Carol S. Dweck, "Mindsets: Developing Talent Through a Growth Mindset," *Olympic Coach* 21, no. 1 (2009): 4-7.

it is worth considering that we do have some control. Belief in control is connected to optimism and positive emotions; whereas loss of control is linked to depression.[15] If we did have control over all things, then it would be enough to hold a growth mindset and then pull ourselves up by our bootstraps. This is the message we send to our kids: "You can be anything you want if you just set your mind to it." It makes sense to teach kids this, because most of the time it is true that if they try, they can do things. There is a reward to effort. It is often true that good things happen when we do good things and try hard. Grit and growth mindset are both correlated with success.[16]

For all the effort that has been put toward getting the growth mindset message out there (see children's coloring books on this topic), rather than believing too little in our ability to control the world, we are likely to believe in that ability too much. To interpret the growth mindset work in its extreme version, everything is achievable with a growth mindset, and there are not any biological or environmental constraints. But people who have failed at something at which they put in a great deal of effort will realize that a growth mindset is not a magic bullet to success. Believing that we possess total control over our lives is a false belief. We often do not have control over major life events. It is easy to believe in personal control until it is gone, until we face a devastating diagnosis, until we are faced with circumstances we did not even consider that have completely derailed the plan. Not everything is within personal control.

Recently, I listened to a podcast in which a Holocaust survivor was explaining what her mother told her before entering Auschwitz. "You don't have control over what will happen to you, but you have control

---

[15]David C. Klein, Ellen Fencil-Morse, and Martin E. Seligman, "Learned Helplessness, Depression, and the Attribution of Failure," *Journal of Personality and Social Psychology* 33, no. 5 (1976): 508-16.

[16]Angela Duckworth and James J. Gross, "Self-Control and Grit," *Current Directions in Psychological Science* 23, no. 5 (2014): 319-25; Dweck, "Mindsets: Developing Talent Through a Growth Mindset."

over your mind."[17] This is also part of the message of Viktor Frankl's *Man's Search for Meaning*, and the underpinning idea of all cognitive behavioral therapy. Having a hopeful attitude is a form of secondary control and is not to be confused with primary control. If the Holocaust survivor had primary control, she could have left the concentration camp. Instead, especially when we do not have primary control, we must give extra attention to our secondary control: what we choose to think about. Exerting secondary control is connected to life satisfaction but not positive emotions, those are reserved for primary control.[18] If we can learn to live according to our values,[19] in conditions that we do not like but do not have control over, we can increase our life satisfaction, which is why mindset matters.

In middle age, I have less primary control over major life events,[20] so I am learning to set up my environment for good fast thinking, and to exert more secondary control through practicing good mindsets. There are so many major life decisions that I have already made that now exert influence on my future decisions that it is easy to feel like the world has become more limited. I will never be a ballerina, a judge, a medical doctor, or a mother to a son. I do not get to exert primary control over those decisions, but I do get to exert secondary control. I get to add the mindset to the circumstances. I can spend time being thankful for the good things that I have in my life and less time thinking about what I do not have. I can spend time asking questions and learning new things instead of arguing with others on the internet. As I notice the limits of my primary control, I can lean into secondary

[17]Maya Shankar, "A Holocaust Survivor's Story (No. 35)," June 27, 2022, in *A Slight Change of Plans*, Puskin Industries, podcast, www.pushkin.fm/podcasts/a-slight-change-of-plans/a-holocaust-survivors-story.

[18]Jasmin Tahmaseb McConatha and Haley M. Huba, "Primary, Secondary, and Emotional Control Across Adulthood," *Current Psychology* 18, no. 2 (1999): 164-70.

[19]Jan Hofer, Athanasios Chasiotis, and Domingo Campos, "Congruence Between Social Values and Implicit Motives: Effects on Life Satisfaction Across Three Cultures," *European Journal of Personality* 20, no. 4 (2006): 305-24.

[20]John B. Morganti et al., "Life-Span Differences in Life Satisfaction, Self-Concept, and Locus of Control," *The International Journal of Aging and Human Development* 26, no. 1 (1988): 45-56.

control. To be accurate about life is to acknowledge that there are many bad things. Having a mindset that denies the bad things in order to maintain self-esteem is what this book is trying to prevent. Instead, we need to acknowledge the bad things and then add the mindset that allows us to best cope with the truth of the situation.

In addition to the clear cases where we do not have control, like cancer diagnoses, there are daily ways that we are being influenced below our awareness. *Priming* is the social psychology word that means activating a file folder below your conscious awareness.[21] Primes are built into our environments. Words, songs, smells, and flags are just a few of the things that can serve as primes. One of my favorite social psychologists began a line of research on priming in which participants did word games with words that would prime different things. His most famous experiment involved priming elderly words (*bingo, retired, grey, wise,* etc.) in a word-find puzzle and then measuring how long it took participants to walk down the hallway. Participants primed with elderly words walked slower. Participants primed with rude words interrupted an experimenter's side conversation more quickly.[22] The idea that words or flags can hijack thought processes below awareness threatens a person's sense of agency. If concentrating on elderly words can slow down my walking speed below my awareness, then any sense I have that I am choosing my own walking speed is an illusion. The only way to reduce the impact of priming on behavior is to be aware of it and set up the environment to prime the things we want it to prime.

For example, on the first day of my statistics class I ask students to write an intention statement regarding what they intend to get out of

[21]J. Bargh, "The Four Horsemen of Automaticity: Awareness, Efficiency, Intentions and Control," in *Handbook of Social Cognition*, vol. 1, ed. Thomas K. Srull and Robert S. Wyer, 2nd ed. (Hillsdale, NJ: Lawrence Erlbaum, 1994), 1-40.

[22]John A. Bargh, Mark Chen, and Lara Burrows, "Automaticity of Social Behavior: Direct Effects of Trait Construct and Stereotype Activation on Action," *Journal of Personality and Social Psychology* 71, no. 2 (1996): 230-44.

the class. They are asked to write about their goals for the class: both in terms of a grade and in terms of knowledge to be used in the future. I then recommend that they put their intention statement somewhere they will regularly see it. This is a deliberate "work hard at statistics" prime that they can put on their dorm room mini fridge. We can set up primes like this across our environments. In a heartbreaking example, overseas domestic workers who gave their employers a picture of their families and a small gift from their home country were less likely to be mistreated and reported higher job satisfaction.[23] This family picture primed humanness for the employers, who then treated their employees with more humanity.

One of the early pioneers of implicit bias research, Mahzarin Banaji, thought that she did not have an implicit preference for White faces over Black ones. Implicit bias, like priming, exists below awareness, and is largely believed to reflect the build-up of associations we receive from our culture (like the perceived association between Black faces and violence). It is useful to think of implicit bias as the result of years of priming that connects two or more ideas to each other. Mahzarin Banaji is an Indian immigrant to the United States who endorses racial equality. Imagine her surprise when she took the implicit association test, a measure of implicit bias that she had a hand in developing, only to find out that she shared a preference for White faces over Black faces.[24] She had to acknowledge that her exposure, like most people living in our culture, favors White faces over Black ones. It is not a reflection of her beliefs about the values of White and Black people. Implicit bias is not racism, but unfortunately, that is what the words translate to in the minds of many people. Implicit bias is the result of learning our culture's association of traits with race. It

---

[23]Toman Barsbai et al., *Picture This: Social Distance and the Mistreatment of Migrant Workers*, National Bureau of Economic Research, 2022.

[24]Kim Mills, "Can We Unlearn Implicit Biases? With Mahzarin Banaji, PhD," in *Speaking of Psychology*, July 2022, American Psychological Association, podcast, www.apa.org/news/podcasts/speaking-of-psychology/implicit-biases.

is not a personal endorsement of superiority, and it is not emotional. Banaji could have just lamented the bias, but what she chose to do was change her environment. She started running screensavers on her computer featuring the faces of inspiring Black people. She tried to change her priming to upset the bias.

Instead of taking the proactive approach like Mahzarin Banaji, it is easier to ignore the idea that there are biases below my awareness that might predispose me to respond in predictable ways based on race. The problem with this is that most people would rather dismiss ideas that threaten their self-esteem rather than pursue accuracy in search of the truth. This can allow us to think that we would never behave in a discriminatory way. When I first introduce the idea of bias, one of the major reasons for students' initial resistance to those ideas is the implication that forces below awareness are the real source of control.[25] As we consider together the evidence of bias and the evidence on how to reduce it, we have to *begin by acknowledging that we do not have all the control* (even though we are biased in wanting to believe that we do), and therefore, we will likely never be unbiased. But our only hope of really exerting control is to try. We can try to improve our thinking by changing the primes in our environment. We can consider when and how we can exert primary and secondary control while acknowledging that there are many situations where human control is only an illusion.

BELIEVING WE ARE MORAL HELPS US FEEL GOOD ABOUT OURSELVES

Not only does it feel good to believe in control, but it also feels good to believe we are moral. *We desperately want to believe that we are moral because it serves our self-esteem.*[26] This bias prevents us from seeing our own moral transgressions clearly; without clarity we cannot

---

[25]Bargh, "The Four Horsemen of Automaticity."
[26]David Dunning, "False Moral Superiority," in *The Social Psychology of Good and Evil*, ed. Arthur G. Miller (New York: Guilford Press, 2016), 171-84.

"remove the speck from your brother's eye" (Matthew 7:3-5). Unfortunately, there are social biases that get in the way of removing our "planks" and in removing the "sawdust" of others. One of the most pernicious is the above-average effect.[27] This effect is a quick and dirty way to feel better that works in nearly every situation. Given that we do not really know who or what is "average," if I do poorly at something, I can console myself with the potentially erroneous belief that my performance is still "above average." As anyone might guess, this approach works best for things about which I do not get regular feedback. It is pretty easy to tell myself that I am above average at getting along with others, but harder to tell myself (and believe it) that I am above average for height. Interestingly, the above-average effect is most pronounced for moral judgments including dimensions like honesty and integrity.

Beyond just the typical above-average effect findings that demonstrate that more than 50 percent of people believe they are above average on a dimension, psychologists had participants rate the desirability of traits, the degree to which they themselves possess those traits, and the degree to which others possess those traits.[28] The difference between the self, others, and desirability is largest for moral traits, which suggests that we are most likely to think that we are above average on moral traits and that others should be working to improve on moral dimensions because those dimensions are very desirable. We see a larger gap in moral dimensions between ourselves and others than we do on other traits like intelligence, attractiveness, or personality factors.

The way to be more accurate in the task described in the preceding paragraph is to assume that we are equally moral compared to those

---

[27]Elanor F. Williams and Thomas Gilovich, "Do People Really Believe They Are Above Average?," *Journal of Experimental Social Psychology* 44, no. 4 (2008): 1121-28.

[28]Ben M. Tappin and Ryan T. McKay, "The Illusion of Moral Superiority," *Social Psychological and Personality Science* 8, no. 6 (2016): 623-31.

around us. In order to increase the match between self-ratings and the self-ratings of others, we should assume similarity. We are best able to predict a person's moral behavior when we predict they will act like we will. As the Bible says, "With the measure you use, it will be measured to you" (Matthew 7:2). What prevents us from assuming others are equally moral? It turns out that we are more likely to perceive that others will behave less morally than we will if the situation presented is more abstract and ambiguous.[29]

Once the situation is described in concrete terms, we are more likely to predict that others will behave just as morally as we will. Once we understand the details of the situation, we are able to adjust the application of moral principles. Since moral decisions are made in concrete situations, our judgments of the morality of those decisions ought to involve the unambiguous details of someone's situation. Let me translate: be careful judging someone without understanding the person's circumstances. The kind of humility that is needed to avoid confirmation bias in forming an opinion on an important issue is the same kind of humility needed to avoid making an incorrect assumption about someone's morality.

Before I had kids, I found the *Supernanny* shows very entertaining.[30] I loved watching how a no-nonsense nanny could come in and help parents with out-of-control kids. I remember how she would teach parents to get their kids to stay in their beds and go to sleep. The show's producers would keep a tally of how many times the parent would have to coerce the child back in bed before he finally went to sleep (sometimes this number went above 100). By the end of the show, the kid could usually go to sleep without getting out of bed. After watching the show, I found it easy to look at those parents and make moral judgments. I remember thinking that those hapless

---

[29]Joris Lammers, "Abstraction Increases Hypocrisy," *Journal of Experimental Social Psychology* 48, no. 2 (2012): 475-80.

[30]*Supernanny*, created by Nick Powell, starring Jo Frost (Ricochet Television, 2005–2011).

parents just needed to work harder at parenting and stop giving in to their kids. Then I had kids. By the time I make it to the end of the day, I am tired, my self-control is nearly exhausted, and it is a lot harder to hold the line when my child might throw a fit if I do not go get her a drink of water. I really do not want to deal with a fit because after the fit, calming her and getting her to sleep will delay even further whatever plans I have for my time that evening. So, I get the water, and I probably throw in a frustrated, angry statement. It is easy to judge the person on TV not knowing all the concrete details; it is easy to let myself off the hook knowing all the concrete details.

One way that I have come to think about humility in moral judgments is to leave room for other ideas, since we do not have all the details. It is not possible to get all the details from a one-hour show like *Supernanny*. We need to seek out sources and ideas with which we disagree to avoid confirmation bias. We also need to leave room to hear other people's ideas, opinions, and concerns to affirm our shared humanity. One of the major ways we leave room is to give time: time to ask more questions, time to consider the opposing arguments, time to question our own beliefs, time to listen beyond the first response, and time before sending the return email. In other words, stop relying on assumptions about others and get explicit concrete data by talking to them.

To pursue accuracy in our assessments of others' morality, psychologists suggest we assume similarity as the default setting;[31] the Bible suggests we "take the plank out of your own eye" before we begin to try to "remove the speck from your brother's eye" (Matthew 7:5). Our self-serving bias prevents us from seeing the log. Self-serving bias is as simple as it sounds. If something good happens, I am a stable genius. If something bad happens, the situation is the cause. This bias prevents me from ever seeing the problem that is in my own eye. I love

---

[31]Tappin and McKay, "The Illusion of Moral Superiority."

this biblical analogy because not only is it metaphorically about vision, but it is also literally about vision. This bias is in fact perceptual; we do not perceive our own fault. To be really accurate and righteous, we need to recognize our moral equivalency in that "all have sinned and fall short of the glory of God" (Romans 3:23) and that "there is no one righteous, not even one" (Romans 3:10).

If we have the plank there, why do we see the speck of sawdust? Turns out we are attuned to negative information—remember the negativity bias from chapter one? Our attention is directed to the slivers of others because the slivers are negative.[32] We are also focused on the slivers of others because the self-serving bias assumes that something about the other person is the real problem. The negative information triggers thinking about someone else's immoral behavior but leaves our own untouched. Whether we are aware of it or not, much of our moral decision-making is relative to our position in the scenario and therefore biased.

The data suggests that the people who cloak themselves in "mission jobs" (that is, pastor, missionary, social worker, and so on), or who happen to think of how moral they are in one area are more likely to behave immorally in another.[33] One argument for the lapse into immoral behavior is that having exhausted the self-control muscle by being especially moral in one area has then opened us up to immoral behavior, just as how starving (or fasting, depending on the moral argument for doing it) might cause us to binge eat at the end of the day rather than consume a healthy meal. Or it could be a process of discounting and score-keeping that we are not even aware we are doing. It may be that doing something moral like donating money to a charity is just like buying a "get out of jail free card" that allows us

---

[32]Paul Rozin and Edward B. Royzman, "Negativity Bias, Negativity Dominance, and Contagion," *Personality and Social Psychology Review* 5, no. 4 (2001): 296-320.
[33]Anna C. Merritt, Daniel A. Effron, and Benoît Monin, "Moral Self-Licensing: When Being Good Frees Us to Be Bad," *Social and Personality Psychology Compass* 4, no. 5 (2010): 344-57.

to ignore someone's email request for volunteers. Remembering this research will make it easier to look at pastors and missionaries and realize that they are likely just as moral as we all are. Their "mission jobs" may have increased the probability of immoral behavior at home where the congregation is not looking. I think it is entirely possible that in my head right now, I am implicitly thinking (but explicitly writing) that it is fine if I spend the rest of the evening tonight watching mindless shows because I have devoted the rest of my day to selfless work.

In 1958, a study was conducted where prizes were given to school children if they reached a particular score on a test, but to do that they would need to cheat.[34] After they either resisted temptation or cheated, their attitudes toward cheating changed. Those who had cheated, not surprisingly, became more lenient about cheating. It is that slippery slope toward immorality that results from having to resolve the dissonance we feel about cheating by justifying our behavior through changing our attitude. In this case, we need other people to help us change our behavior instead of our attitudes so we can return to moral behavior. This is what I tell myself before I confront a student who has plagiarized or cheated. My confrontation is for their long-term benefit because the intense shame of the dissonance will not merely allow for an attitude change, but will also invoke a behavior change. When I confront students, I often watch shame flood their features, and to their credit, most students confess and apologize. Students are especially ashamed and likely to confess when they know they have another class to take with me in the future. I am the only social psychology and research methods instructor and so, if students have only taken one of these courses, they know they will need to make amends with me in order to have a good experience in the next class. Confrontation works best in ongoing relationships.

---

[34]Judson Mills, "Changes in Moral Attitudes Following Temptation," *Journal of Personality* 26, no. 4 (1958): 517-31.

While what happened to the cheaters in the experiment is important, I am more interested in what happens to the child who has the opportunity to cheat, but then doesn't. That child becomes even more opposed to cheating than they were before. They forget that they were ever tempted and are likely thinking, *If I can resist temptation, there is no excuse for anyone else not to resist it.* This thinking is what underpins moral hypocrisy. The failure to realize that we are on the same page morally as other people, or the failure to acknowledge the possibility of personal moral failure under any circumstances is a dangerous place to try to pitch a tent. Like the student who cheats and finds future cheating easier, the tendency to judge others harshly gets stronger with each successive experience of resisting temptation.

There are times when I read the Gospels and identify most strongly with the Pharisees or the elder brother in the prodigal son parable. I look at others from my lofty moral perch and provide recommendations rather than love. I am shocked, angry, and judgmental about the blatant racism I see in the church. I can spend an entire conversation on what I think is wrong with the present-day church. The irony is that from that self-righteous position, the view is the most biased. Moral hypocrisy is most likely to emerge when we judge and think about ourselves in ways that are ambiguous, desirable, and abstract. We would be more accurate to make judgments in ways that are specific and concrete. For example, it is wonderful to think about myself as kind, generous, and loving without having to acknowledge the specific and concrete situation in which I did not volunteer to bring snacks to soccer practice. The second half of that sentence is easy to confirm as unequivocally true, whereas the first half of that sentence is open for interpretation.

The journey I have taken as a Christian and a social psychologist has been to recognize that intellectual and moral humility is the only path forward if we want to pursue accuracy in our assessment of our own morality. We need to lean on the desire we have to be accurate and righteous to help us remember that our file folders are incomplete. Humility, defined as lacking pride or having a spirit of submission, is something that I find elusive—like a state of complete purity. Humility feels like altruism, in that the minute I think I have it, I obviously do not. To be less biased, *we need the humility it takes to assume others are equally moral.* So instead of trying to attain "humility," which feels unattainable, it is important to practice humble behaviors. For example, intellectual humility means listening to opposing views and reading information that challenges our own perspectives. It means admitting that we could be wrong. It means waiting an extra day or more to send an email because we recognize that our first reaction might not be the right one.

BELIEVING WE ARE BETTER THAN OTHERS HELPS US FEEL GOOD ABOUT OURSELVES

In addition to believing we have more control than we do and that we are more moral than others, another manifestation of a self-bias is believing that we are generally better than others by comparison. We engage in upward social comparisons when we compare ourselves to people who are better off than we are, but this can either demoralize us if their success is unattainable or inspire us if their success is attainable.[35] Downward social comparisons involve comparing ourselves to someone worse off than we are. The process of downward social comparison boosts self-esteem.[36] This is another "quick and dirty" way to quickly boost self-esteem. It is like a shot of sugar when I am hungry. No matter how bad something is in my life, I can think of some situation that is worse, as measured by the "Pain Olympics" in which we are all competing. When I get a flat tire, I can be glad my car is not totaled. When I get a headache, I can be thankful I do not have

---

[35]Penelope Lockwood and Ziva Kunda, "Superstars and Me: Predicting the Impact of Role Models on the Self," *Journal of Personality and Social Psychology* 73, no. 1 (1997): 91-103.

[36]Jerry Suls, René Martin, and Ladd Wheeler, "Social Comparison: Why, with Whom, and with What Effect?," *Current Directions in Psychological Science* 11, no. 5 (2002): 159-63.

brain cancer. *We want to feel good about ourselves, so we are thirsty for downward social comparisons to get a quick boost to self-esteem.*

Glenn Boozan recently published a book titled *There Are Moms Way Worse Than You*,[37] which is a book about animal moms who do despicable things to their offspring. Even cross-species downward comparisons can make us feel better about ourselves. Whether I am a better mom than a baboon is obviously irrelevant except that it can make me feel better for a quick minute. This behavior starts to seem a little bit worse when we compare ourselves to a specific person. "I may not have gotten an A on the test, but at least I did not get a score as low as my friend Madison." After hearing the definition of social comparisons, nearly everyone thinks social comparisons are bad. Constantly measuring ourselves relative to others must be bad. Like everyone else, I have been engaging in social comparisons all my life, but mostly these comparisons take place in my head.

About ten years ago, I met someone who is the personification of Kristin Wiig's SNL character named Penelope, who is constantly one-upping people. If you do not remember her, here is a typical scene. In one sketch, Penelope was volunteering at a soup kitchen on Thanksgiving. The organizer of the soup kitchen stated that she found out that her relatives had come over on the Mayflower, to which Penelope replied that her relatives "had come over on the Aprilflower so they had arrived one month earlier."[38] I had never expected to meet anyone in real life who one-ups as much as Penelope did. Like Penelope, if I told her I had just had an article published in a particular journal, she would state that she had published at least three articles in that journal in the past year. If I mentioned that a tree in my yard was flowering, she would tell me that horticulturists from Purdue were coming to study the trees in her yard. If I told her that I found a four-leaf clover,

---

[37]Glenn Boozan and Priscilla Witte, *There Are Moms Way Worse Than You: Irrefutable Proof That You Are Indeed a Fantastic Parent* (New York: Workman, 2022).
[38]*Saturday Night Live*, "Penelope," November 20, 2010, on NBC.

she would tell me that she can spot four-leaf clovers while driving down the road at sixty-five miles per hour. If I told her that I had served in the military, she would tell me that she had trained snipers in Ukraine. Now, is this person mentally okay? The answer is clearly no. Something was definitely wrong. She has moved from university to university because universities eventually figure out that she is not telling the truth. It usually takes a few months, or even years, before she is let go. This person even has a TEDx talk. This is an extreme case, but there are less extreme versions of this.

There are people that I rarely see because every conversation holds the possibility for emotional shrapnel. You know what I mean. I want to tell my good news, but the other person fails to celebrate and one-ups me instead. Having just been one-upped, I walk away from the conversation thinking, "If that is how you respond when I have good news, I would rather not talk to you." The level of pettiness in such constant one-upping causes us to withdraw from the one-upper. In the past, I think I would have placed all the blame on the one-upper as the culprit in that situation—but let's dive deeper into the self-esteem maintenance mechanisms that are in play on both sides of the conversation.

The person who is one-upping is probably doing it to boost self-esteem. It is a classic form of downward social comparison to constantly point out how we are better off than someone else. We all do it, but we do not all do it to someone's face. There is some self-esteem deficit that is driving the behavior, and it has social consequences. No one wants to be around Penelope, or the lying professor, or the one-upping friend. I do not have the data, but I am going to guess that they are not aware of the social cost they are paying, because instead of asking the one-uppers, "Why are you one-upping me?" most people decide to avoid them. This might be an appropriate response to a stranger, but if this one-upper is family, we owe it to them to point it out and try to help. There is a misplaced identity that is driving the need to prove their value in one-upping you. There is also a self-esteem issue on the part of the person who collects the rude statements rather than confronting the one-upper. Holding on to rude statements a one-upper made is petty. We need to see the one-uppers for who they are. One-uppers are people like us who are trying to feel good about themselves but might need some help building a solid foundation of self-esteem. The downward social comparison provides a quick and dirty boost to self-esteem, but it will not sustain self-esteem over the long-haul no matter how much we use it.[39]

On the other side of social comparison, not only do we engage in downward social comparisons, but we also compare ourselves to people who are better off.[40] The data suggest that we engage in social comparison automatically and with whomever is nearby, so that would necessarily include some people who are doing better than we are. It is adaptive to engage in upward social comparison because comparing ourselves with someone ahead of us can be a source of inspiration.[41] A lot has been made of celebrity culture, even within Christian circles with famous pastors and authors.[42] If we were constantly engaging in downward social comparisons with people, we would not elevate these celebrity pastors; instead, they are a source of upward comparisons that lead to inspiration. We like to celebrate people who are doing things well.

The downside of upward comparisons is that they can be depressing if we are constantly comparing ourselves to people who are better off but do not present an attainable model.[43] They have something we

---

[39]Frederick X. Gibbons and Meg Gerrard, "Effects of Upward and Downward Social Comparison on Mood States," *Journal of Social and Clinical Psychology* 8, no. 1 (1989): 14-31.

[40]Lisa G. Aspinwall and Shelley E. Taylor, "Effects of Social Comparison Direction, Threat, and Self-Esteem on Affect, Self-Evaluation, and Expected Success," *Journal of Personality and Social Psychology* 64, no. 5 (1993): 708–22.

[41]Pascal Huguet et al., "Social Comparison Choices in the Classroom: Further Evidence for Students' Upward Comparison Tendency and Its Beneficial Impact on Performance," *European Journal of Social Psychology* 31, no. 5 (2001): 557-78, https://doi.org/10.1002/ejsp.81.

[42]Katelyn Beaty, *Celebrities for Jesus: How Personas, Platforms, and Profits Are Hurting the Church* (Grand Rapids, MI: Brazos, 2022).

[43]Lockwood and Kunda, "Superstars and Me."

want but can never hope to attain, a situation that is very depressing. If, however, we are not trying to attain the status celebrities have, we might still feel inspired by their general model of excellence. For example, someone might feel inspired by the excellence of the work of Steve Jobs but not make any effort to follow in his specific footsteps. In the abstract, nothing is wrong with social comparison, either upward or downward, but the reason many of my students choose to write about social comparison as the topic of their final papers in my social psychology class is that they are intimately familiar with the negative effects of upward social comparison. It breeds jealousy. They are also familiar with the negative effects of downward social comparisons. It breeds moral superiority and hypocrisy. These very negative effects are what stand out to the students studying this topic, so they end up writing papers that suggest that we should end social comparisons altogether and that the Christian perspective supports the eradication of social comparisons.

On the surface, yes, I agree that social comparisons have these negative effects. If I am constantly trying to keep up with the wealthy people around me and engaging in social comparison to justify foolish spending and superficial posturing, then social comparison is driving bad behavior. Using other people as a primary metric for the value of life is mostly bad because there are so few people that are providing an inspiring example. But reading biographies of inspirational figures is a healthy practice. Reading the Bible looking for inspiration from Jesus as a holy (although unattainable) example is a healthy practice. The real reason that most of us feel some ambivalence about social comparison is that it cannot substitute for the real self-esteem development process that results from having a secure identity. A secure identity results from a well-developed worldview and living in a way that is consistent with that worldview. *We need to pursue accuracy and righteousness to avoid the pitfall of trying to feel good about ourselves through downward social comparison.*

YOU ARE WORSE THAN GOD AND EQUAL TO OTHERS

My best answer for how to reduce a self-bias is *repetitive reflection on the self and on God, and on the proper position of the self relative to God and to others*. What I mean is that we have to start with thinking about who we are as children of God and sinners saved by grace. Next, we need to think about who God is. This is followed by comparing the self to God. If we are measuring the self relative to God on any dimension, the distance between God's score and our score is huge. I frequently think of the distance between me and God as the distance between the earth and the moon, but I know that that particular distance is just an imaginary stand-in for "huge distance." If I sit in that posture of recognition of God's awesomeness, omniscience, omnipresence, and unfathomable nature, I start to see myself more clearly. I see the limits to my thinking and my understanding, and I am humbled. I think we need to imagine and meditate on that distance between God and us daily.

My youngest daughter recently helped me to put myself in the right perspective. We were visiting a friend's lake house on a beautiful August day, and I was rocking her in a hammock. It felt idyllic and I was transported to some of my own happy childhood memories when I felt free of worry. I started singing "He's Got the Whole World in His Hands"[44] with my daughter. I got to the verse where "He's got the itty-bitty babies in His hands" and then asked my five-year-old to make up her own verses. She sang, "He's got the itty-bitty people in His hands." Her next verse was the "itty-bitty trees" and in every subsequent verse something was "itty-bitty." In that moment, I thought she had it just about right. Relative to God's hands, it is all itty-bitty.

The next distance to measure is between me and other people. This is a social comparison, but the social comparison is different when it comes after a social comparison with God. Once you have

---

[44]Laurie London, "He's Got the Whole World in His Hands" (Parlophone, 1957).

established the distance between the self and God, this distance between you and me is tiny. It is like standing on the subway car at rush
hour with someone touching nearly every surface of my body,
probably even closer. We are so much more alike in our thinking and
understanding that it does not seem worth comparing whatever
small ways one of us might be superior to the other. It would be like
measuring who gets off the subway first. It is so close in time that it
does not matter. Those upward and downward comparisons have
lost their power. In our deeper identity, we are all children of God
and sinners saved by grace.

I often think that God will make it clear in heaven that we spent
way too much time on earth measuring the distances between each
other instead of loving each other in our shared humanity. Too often
the default positioning is to think that God is a lot like me, and other
people are very different from me. In the morning, before I leave my
bed, I start my day by imagining who I am as a child of God and
sinner saved by grace, who God is, the distance between me and God,
and then the distance between me and others. Setting up these posi-
tions and social comparisons at the beginning of the day is a practice
that can allow us to put the other social comparisons in their proper
perspective. I can acknowledge the ways that I am different from
others in the sizing-up process, but those differences do not have to
affect my value because I have already established that relative to God,
our value as his children and as sinners is the same.[45]

If, however, instead of spending the beginning of the day thinking
of our secure identity and positioning the self to God and then the
self to others, we start our days with a dose of Instagram, it may have
the exact opposite effect of the joy and peace we get from proper positioning to God and others. The data are starting to emerge that more
time on social media can be linked to depression and the potential

---

[45]I am not arguing that all sins are equivalent or that sin is acceptable, but that our value and
identity is the same as other humans.

mediator is social comparison.[46] If what we do on social media is compare our looks, our possessions, and the coolness of our lifestyles to people online, we have just allowed some of the most superficial distinctions between people to be the ways in which we think about others. These are superficial file folders that we have just opened. This divides us rather than unites us. I do not argue for an all or nothing type of approach to social media, but I would argue that if we engage in social comparisons on social media (pretty hard not to do that), we need to first take some of the emotional weight away from the comparisons, which is what the positioning of self to God and self to others should do.

Engaging in this positioning practice is important because it sets the motivation on being accurate. What I mean is, once we think about how much higher, bigger, and better God is, we have recognized that we are not righteous or accurate in our thinking. But we are now positioned to *pursue* accuracy and righteousness in order to take on the "mind of Christ" (1 Corinthians 2:16). Thinking about our similarity to other people in having a shared identity as children of God and sinners saved by grace diffuses the need to prove that we are valuable as a way to feel good about ourselves. *Once you have met the motivation to feel good about yourself, you are freed up to pursue accuracy and righteousness.*[47] The positioning exercise sets up our thinking for the day to be less biased. The rest of this book is dedicated to conditions and strategies that can help us keep the important file folders open throughout the day so that the lens we use to see the world is one that accurately reflects our position relative to God and others. We have covered the biases that most affect the self to build a self-concept that is less biased and more secure,

---

[46]Helmut Appel, Alexander L. Gerlach, and Jan Crusius, "The Interplay Between Facebook Use, Social Comparison, Envy, and Depression," *Current Opinion in Psychology* 9 (2016): 44-49.

[47]On accuracy, see Lauren Eskreis-Winkler and Ayelet Fishbach, "You Think Failure Is Hard? So Is Learning from It," *Perspectives on Psychological Science* 17, no. 6 (2022): 1511-24.

but now we have to consider how to *think* and live in that less-biased identity.

CHAPTER THREE SUMMARY

We filter new information through a self-bias, which can lead us to sacrifice accuracy for self-esteem. The self-bias shows up in our desire to believe that we have more control than we actually have, that we are more moral than we actually are, and that we are better than others when we actually are not. We need to have our self-esteem needs met through affirmation of a secure identity as children of God and sinners saved by grace, so we can be freed up to pursue accuracy. Reducing a self-bias requires repetitive reflection on the proper position of the self relative to God and to others.

APPLICATION: UNBIASED NUDGES

- Acknowledge that you have a self-bias. Look for examples of when it shows up in your life.

- Acknowledge that you have less control than you think you have. Consider how you can exert control by changing the primes in your environment.

- Acknowledge that most people are just as moral as you are. Consider the way concrete and abstract statements are relevant to your judgments of morality.

- Acknowledge that you regularly engage in social comparison. Be thankful for the good things that exist in your life.

- Position your capacity, morality, and capabilities relative to God's. Next, position your capacity, morality, and capabilities relative to another human. Meditate on this positioning and its implications.

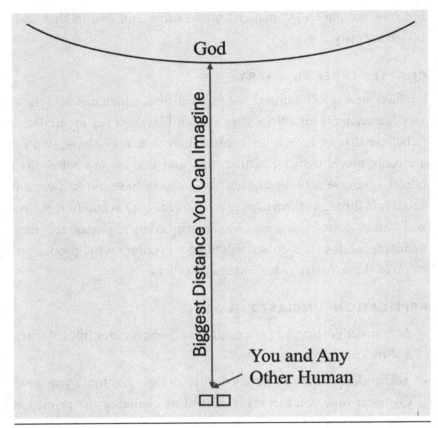

Figure 3.1. Your position relative to God and to others

FOUR

LESS-BIASED SLOW THINKING

THINKING ABOUT THE SELF relative to God and the self relative to others is an important starting point to reduce bias, and it would be beneficial to think about this positioning all the time because it would satisfy our need to feel good about ourselves as well as activate the pursuit of accuracy. Realistically though, we are probably going to have to do other things in our day, like figure out what to eat and decide where to get that food, which will take some amount of thinking about other things. A day will likely consist of millions of slow thoughts, the kind of thoughts that you would generate if I were to ask you right now what you are thinking about. These are the only thoughts that we have easy access to, and they are the only thoughts that most of us even acknowledge as thoughts. While it is not possible to put a number on them, these deliberate slow thoughts are likely only a tiny fraction of our thoughts. The great majority of our thoughts are happening below our own awareness, and only later influence our conscious thoughts.[1] For example, you may not be able to explain how you detected the annoyance in your mother's voice or how you knew that your friend needed a hug at that moment. You are acting based on impressions and intuitions that you have no explanation for most of the time. These are fast thoughts. Most books on thinking are designed to help improve slow thinking and therefore will not have nearly the impact we think they will, because we aren't good at accounting for all the fast

---

[1]Daniel Kahneman, *Thinking Fast and Slow* (New York: Penguin, 2011), 20-26.

thinking we are routinely doing. This chapter will start with the typical focus on improving deliberate thinking but has the goal of making good slow-thinking practices so routine that they eventually become fast thinking.

Controlled thinking gives us the benefit of taking time to align our behavior with our values. There is ample evidence to demonstrate that people feel better when they are behaving in ways that are consistent with deeply held values.[2] Consider that high self-esteem is established, according to terror management theory,[3] by building a coherent worldview and living in ways that are consistent with that worldview. If automatic thoughts are leading to behavior that is not consistent with our values, we may need to practice better slow thoughts in order to eventually replace the faulty fast thoughts. This is the work it takes to break an addiction like stress eating. For example, you will probably need to use the information from the next chapter to change your environment to facilitate less stress eating by removing food, rewarding relaxation, and surrounding yourself with people who don't stress eat—but you also need to combine these practices with some deliberate effort to replace the thoughts that were connected to the stress eating in the first place. You may need to identify the times when you tell yourself that "eating will make you feel better" and replace it with "talking to a friend will make you feel better." This chapter will *help you figure out how to practice good slow thinking in order to build better fast thoughts in the future.*

At this point, ideally you are excited to pursue accuracy instead of just believing you are right. Now it's important to employ strategies to pursue more accurate, less-biased slow thinking because we are most comfortable seeking information that confirms what we already

---

[2] Kelly G. Wilson et al., "The Valued Living Questionnaire: Defining and Measuring Valued Action Within a Behavioral Framework," *The Psychological Record* 60, no. 2 (2010): 249-72.

[3] J. Greenberg, T. Pyszczynski, and S. Solomon, "The Causes and Consequences of a Need for Self-Esteem: A Terror Management Theory," *Public Self and Private Self* (1986): 189-212.

think (remember the confirmation bias).[4] The default setting is not to pursue accuracy but to congratulate ourselves for already achieving it. We seek out confirming information because it makes us feel right and feel good about ourselves for being right. These two primary motivations (being right and feeling good about ourselves) create a powerful elixir when they are combined. If people find comfort in agreement, this "yes bias"[5] will lead them to hold on to agreement for as long as possible. If ideas can cause us to feel right and good about ourselves, people will believe them as long as possible, even in the face of disconfirming evidence. It feels even better when we can hold those beliefs with certainty bordering on dogmatism.[6] That confidence in the rightness of an idea makes the world a predictable and controllable place. Thus, the belief in the just world is strengthened.[7] Having a perception of control also feels good and comfortable. There is a lot of motivation to maintain a strong and integrated belief system. This paragraph is my best attempt to summarize how people actually think, but this is not how they *should* think. *Instead of wanting to be right, we should pursue accuracy.* If identity is not tied to holding the "right" beliefs because the self-schema is more accurately organized around being a child of God and sinner saved by grace, there is room to be wrong, which will lead to greater accuracy in the future. We need some strategies to pursue accuracy instead of settling for what seems right to us.

In the next chapter, I will describe conditions that we can create in our environment to help us pursue accuracy. These are things that we have some primary control over, such as choosing friends who both love and challenge our thinking. The current chapter focuses more on

---

[4]Raymond S. Nickerson, "Confirmation Bias: A Ubiquitous Phenomenon in Many Guises," *Review of General Psychology* 2, no. 2 (1998): 175-220.

[5]Daniel T. Gilbert, "How Mental Systems Believe," *American Psychologist* 46, no. 2 (1991): 107-19.

[6]Joshua J. Clarkson et al., "Does Attitude Certainty Beget Self-Certainty?," *Journal of Experimental Social Psychology* 45, no. 2 (2009): 436-39.

[7]Melvin J. Lerner, "The Belief in a Just World," in *The Belief in a Just World: A Fundamental Decision* (Boston: Springer, 1980), 9-30.

the secondary control we have and how the mindset that we bring to a question will guide our process in answering it. Adam Grant makes the argument that we should think like a scientist, when most of us reason like lawyers.[8] If we thought like scientists, we would be designing experiments to test hypotheses and would need evidence to support the hypotheses before we chose to believe in their veracity. We would be pursuing accuracy. Instead, like lawyers, we have a defendant that we represent, and we look for evidence to support our case. We want to prove we are right. For example, consider the article titled, "Sweatshop Labor Is Wrong Unless the Shoes Are Cute: Cognition Can Both Help and Hurt Moral Motivated Reasoning."[9] I tell students not to include titles in writing, but I love the title so much that I want to include it. I have just engaged in some moral reasoning in order to justify the breaking of my own rule. My moral or good academic writing principle is "Don't ever include journal article titles in the body of the paper." When I am applying rules to others, I am very likely to apply the rule absolutely. In the article mentioned above, the authors find that we are more willing to endorse sweatshop labor justifications for a vacation for ourselves than if the vacation were for a friend. In the case that *we* get to enjoy a Caribbean beach vacation, we are more willing to excuse poor labor practices, but we would not let our friends get away with this same excuse.

We behave like lawyers; we want to go on a beach vacation or include a title in our writing, so now we need to find the arguments to justify it. We start with the arguments. We don't withhold judgment and stage an experiment like scientists. Interestingly, this motivated reasoning is not a fully automatic process. When the authors added a cognitive load manipulation where participants had to memorize the

---

[8] Adam Grant, *Think Again: The Power of Knowing What You Don't Know* (New York: Penguin Books, 2023), 18-20.

[9] Neeru Paharia, Kathleen D. Vohs, and Rohit Deshpandé, "Sweatshop Labor Is Wrong Unless the Shoes Are Cute: Cognition Can Both Help and Hurt Moral Motivated Reasoning," *Organizational Behavior and Human Decision Processes* 121, no. 1 (2013): 81-88.

number 7264281 and then make judgments about justifications for questionable labor practices at a Caribbean resort, those under cognitive load did not endorse the justifications. It seems that the mental loopholes we create to justify our behavior take cognitive effort, and therefore in these situations, we might behave more ethically if there is a cognitive load.

In this case, if the default setting is to apply a moral principle, adding load can reduce the potentially negative exception-making effects of motivated reasoning. So, where do the cute shoes factor into the experiments? The details of their experiments, reveal that they do not, in fact, manipulate the cuteness of shoes, but instead manipulated the desirability of the shoes based on how much of a discount the buyer received (75 percent off a pair of Nikes that retail at $175.00 or just 5 percent off the same pair). As might be expected, participants are more likely to make justifications for sweatshops when the shoes are on sale. I guess the authors of this study were motivated to stretch the truth of their title because "sweatshop labor is wrong unless the shoes are on sale" doesn't have the same ring to it, but I'm wondering if they might judge their friends more harshly than themselves for the same title.

In another more seriously themed experiment, related to the "guilty person" file folder in chapter one, Saul Kassin looks at the ability to detect deception in confessions.[10] There is an entire body of research on the conditions under which false confessions can happen, and yet many people have a hard time believing that anyone under any condition would confess to a crime that they did not commit. Kassin has conducted many cleverly designed experiments around the creation of false confessions, including one in which college students and detectives are participants who need to judge which confessions are real

---

[10]Saul M. Kassin, Christian A. Meissner, and Rebecca J. Norwick, "'I'd Know a False Confession If I Saw One': A Comparative Study of College Students and Police Investigators," *Law and Human Behavior* 29, no. 2 (2005): 211-27.

versus which are fake. No one is very good at the task (accurate at chance levels) but, sadly and not surprisingly, detectives are worse at the task than college students and are also more confident in their decisions. More confident and less accurate is not a good combination. The explanation Kassin gives for the poor performance of detectives is that they hold stronger views about the accuracy of confessions under all circumstances. This motivation to believe that confessions are accurate (wanting to be right) creates a bias that makes it harder to distinguish between false and real confessions.

In order to pursue accuracy and reduce bias, we need to *acknowledge our motives*. What I mean is, I need to acknowledge that I want to buy the shoes, so I'm going to look for reasons to buy them. I need to acknowledge that I want to go on vacation, so I'm going to look for a good explanation for why I should. If I were a detective, I would need to acknowledge that my "guilty person" file folder biases me to assume confessions are real. There are things that we want to believe whether they are true or not. We need to take a minute and acknowledge how what we *want* to be true might influence our ability to judge what is *actually true*. Once I have acknowledged what I want to be true, I can renew my desire to set that aside to pursue accuracy. Once I acknowledge that I am viewing the labor practices differently because I want to go on vacation, I can see the failure of moral reasoning for what it is.

GOOD THINKING EMBRACES UNCERTAINTY

If, as I argue in the preceding section, we are motivated thinkers who are mostly concerned with finding arguments to support what we really want to believe, perhaps it makes sense to conclude that rational objective thought is impossible. We might be tempted to conclude that truth is relative, and all decisions are equivalent. It's also possible to make the same argument that a person should favor accuracy over self-esteem once self-esteem needs are met. Perhaps accuracy is not an achievable goal, even after we acknowledge and set aside our motivations, because it is just not possible to have enough information on any topic to really claim that we are accurate in any assessment. Rather than pursuing accuracy, since accuracy is not achievable, we might as well pursue feeling good. If this is the line of argument that you embrace, I would urge you to consider that we aren't just motivated to be right, but also to be righteous. To be righteous, a person must *pursue accuracy* even when perfection is out of reach. It is the attempt at accuracy that is required for righteousness to exist.

One of the benefits of parenting is that I am confronted with doubt and forced into intellectual humility by the incessant questions of my children. As a parent, I have dealt with the frustration of trying to explain something to someone who really cannot understand something no matter how well I explain it to them. I am not unlike that child. There are things that I don't have the background knowledge to understand, and like a child, it might take years to get me to that point. Given the length of my life, there will not be time to gain understanding of many, many topics. Part of the resistance people experience in both recognizing and acknowledging bias is rooted in the difficulty we have with all our cognitive limitations. It is hard to know in which ways and to what degree I am limited. The famous Kruger-Dunning effect demonstrates how it takes knowledge to even recognize that you don't have knowledge.[11] In their experiment the participants who perform the worst are also the worst at recognizing their own ability. We must have some level of competence to even judge our own level of competence. The antidote to the "Don't know enough to know what I don't know" problem is to have someone keep asking follow-up questions. It's easy to think we understand how toilets work until someone (like a child) asks the follow-up, "Why does it do that?" after the first explanation. In light of all the topics

---

[11]Justin Kruger and David Dunning, "Unskilled and Unaware of It: How Difficulties in Recognizing One's Own Incompetence Lead to Inflated Self-Assessments," *Journal of Personality and Social Psychology* 77, no. 6 (1999): 1121-34.

about which most of us know very little, let's start to embrace doubt with a mindset of intellectual humility; otherwise, we can't give the intellectually honest answer—"I don't know the answer to that; let me get back to you later"—to many of life's questions.

Perhaps now you are convinced that there are biases preventing us from accurately approaching information. You are ready to embrace doubt and intellectual humility and are now planning to write pro and con lists with corresponding footnotes to data sources for every decision and belief. I would say, not all decisions and beliefs require this, but for those that do, please also conclude your list with a probabilistic estimate of your confidence in the accuracy of your decision. The reason why we make a pro and con list and take time to think through a major decision is because we are uncertain. It's not possible to know how often things will turn out a certain way with exact precision, so it might feel strange at first to attach a probability to a decision. Even if it feels inaccurate to be placing a numeric probability on an outcome, it's not less accurate than placing a non-numeric prediction (that is, "this will turn out great") without acknowledging that is what you are doing. Predictions are by their very nature imperfect. By adding a number, we are taking an implicit non-numeric prediction, and making it explicit. When we don't add probabilities, we are more likely to give "all or nothing" estimates to our decisions. By adding numeric probabilities, we are more likely to acknowledge the nuance present, which will result in a more accurate assessment. Cognitive psychologist and poker champion Annie Duke argues, "Even if our assessment results in a wide range, like the chances of a particular scenario occurring being between 20% and 80%, that is still better than not guessing at all."[12]

In her book *Thinking in Bets*, Annie Duke describes one experiment that pits the traditional scientific approach against a poker

---

[12]Annie Duke, *Thinking in Bets: Making Smarter Decisions When You Don't Have All the Facts* (New York: Penguin, 2019), 210.

player approach.[13] Scientists rely on peer review to distinguish between what warrants publication and what doesn't. To judge the likelihood of the replication of a series of experiments, scientists in related fields were asked to judge which experiments would replicate after rereading the original articles. These scientists were right 58 percent of the time. When asked to make monetary bets about which experiments would replicate, these same experts were right 71 percent of the time. Arguably, there was a betting element in both conditions, where one's professional reputation is on the line, but adding the explicit bet in the second condition led to greater accuracy.

Based on these and other results, Annie Duke urges us to seek greater accuracy and objectivity in our decision-making, by rewarding the kind of behavior that will increase it.[14] Specifically, she suggests that we should seek the rewards of "being a good credit-giver, a good mistake-admitter, a good finder-of-mistakes-in-good-outcomes, a good learner, and (as a result) a good decision-maker."[15] She suggests that you find a group of others who are willing to critique your decision-making processes. To provide an objective critique, they need to hear your story without the outcome, because outcome bias will likely taint the critique. Outcome bias is the idea that most people only judge the quality of the decision by the outcome.[16] If it was a good outcome, then it resulted from a good process. If it was a bad outcome, it emanated from a bad process. When explicitly stated, this is obviously false, and yet few of us take time to really critique the process that leads to good outcomes. We need to critique the process of both good and bad outcomes if we want to learn how to improve future decision-making. There is a lot outside of our control and a lot

---

[13]Duke, *Thinking in Bets*, 149-50.

[14]Corinne L. Townsend and Evan Heit, "Judgments of Learning and Improvement," *Memory & Cognition* 39, no. 2 (2010): 204-16.

[15]Duke, *Thinking in Bets*, 108.

[16]Jonathan Baron and John C. Hershey, "Outcome Bias in Decision Evaluation," *Journal of Personality and Social Psychology* 54, no. 4 (1988): 569-79.

that is within control; taking time to distinguish the process from the outcome explicitly rather than in a self-serving manner is how learning takes place.

Adding confidence ratings, like adding probabilities, can lead to greater accuracy. It is helpful to recognize that I have a low confidence rating for my knowledge of God. I remember this feeling distinctly as an undergraduate in a class titled something like "Theological Philosophy" or "Philosophical Theology." The class was about whether God was even knowable. If the answer is, "Yes, God is knowable," then the next question is, "What is God like?" I remember very little of the specifics of this course (even the name of the class is a question in my mind), but I remember the overall conclusion that I cannot fully know God, and what I can know about God is limited by language and experience. Therefore, thinking about Scripture leads me to the view that Scripture is written in a way that we can understand imperfectly but not entirely literally. That Scripture is not to be read and understood as entirely literal leads back to the uncomfortable feeling that I cannot be sure of what I know or what I read.

I want to argue that both thinking about God as hard to know and the Bible as hard to understand (because it is not entirely literal) is both uncomfortable and good. Imagine stating explicitly, "I understand God fully; there is nothing about God that I don't understand." This is an outrageous statement, but I wonder how often I operate from a perspective that assumes that I already know what God thinks about something (and that what God thinks is in agreement with what I think). Likewise, the Bible being difficult to understand is what keeps me coming back to think more deeply. A regular recognition of the unknowable nature of God and complexity of Scripture should be part of the practice of humility, curiosity, openness, and awe. Sitting in prayer recognizing that God is beyond understanding and that Scripture is God-breathed ought to be a de-biasing force, because we know that humility, curiosity, openness, and awe are linked to reductions in bias.

Not everything is as deep and steeped in meaning as the nature of God and Scripture, but many things are impossible to fully know and understand. When I discuss bias in class, students are occasionally distraught that we can't absolutely know things, so they ask me how I know that what I am saying is true. My response is that I am not sure that what I am saying is true in an absolute sense. In the past I gave an estimate that I now think is even higher than is likely, that 80 percent of what I say in class is true. First, most of the experimental data I present is based on the idea that 5 percent of the time, the data could have turned out that way randomly, rather than because the theory is true. So even if I were accurately reporting only experimental research, I would be wrong 5 percent of the time. Given the constraints of my own memory, the possibility of my own fallible interpretation of the results, combined with contextual factors on a given day, I gave the high estimate that 80 percent of what I said in class was accurate.

If I can really only give a confidence rating of 80 percent on the topic about which I have received the most education, is there anything that can be known with more certainty? The only appropriate answer I can give to that question is "I'm not sure." First, I have to say 'I'm not sure," because how can one really be certain of one's own certainty or lack of certainty? It's entirely circular. As mentioned previously, I am now of the opinion (based on data) that we should give confidence ratings for statements. For example, when one of my friends was dating her now husband, he said he was "80 percent in favor of marrying her and 20 percent against it." Now, I'm going to guess that you are as scandalized by this statement as I was at the time. In my twenties I thought someone who wanted to marry you should be 100 percent sure; now, I don't believe that it is possible to be 100 percent sure, and anyone who claims to be doesn't know the person they are considering well enough to recognize their faults. I now think that he was a person of high integrity who was willing to share his real feelings. When my husband wanted to have another baby, even though I was originally against it, I decided to think about it, pray about it, and give it a number. I will admit to being highly swayed by his argument that at the end of his life he might regret not having another child, so I gave him my confidence rating. I was 80 percent in favor of it and 20 percent against it. We did not have another baby, so I can't be 100 percent devastated.

A few years ago, some colleagues and I started asking students to give confidence ratings for their answers to quiz questions.[17] We incentivized accuracy on the ratings by giving and taking away points. For example, if they got the quiz question right and had given themselves a high confidence rating, they got two points for the question. If, however, they got the question wrong and had high confidence, they lost two points for the question. If they got the question right, but had low confidence, they got one point. This incentivizing of metacognition (thinking about our own thinking) led to greater accuracy over the course of the class and led to improved scores overall. The process of learning to calibrate confidence and accuracy doesn't happen naturally; the addition of the ratings and the incentivizing of accuracy were essential to the calibration process.[18] In life, we can easily explain away circumstances that don't conform to our predictions, which means that we don't ever really practice calibrating, but the practice of adding confidence ratings on decisions may be very helpful in improving accuracy.

Let's return to the question of what is knowable about God. That number is low in my mind. When I am presented with theological questions, I should access that number (let's give it 5 percent) and

---

[17] A. C. Hall, C. J. Devers, E. E. Devers, and T. Chen, "Metacognitive Accuracy Predicts Course Performance" (Poster, Association for Psychological Science 31st Annual Convention, Washington, DC, May 2019).

[18] Daniel L. Dinsmore and Meghan M. Parkinson, "What Are Confidence Judgments Made of? Students' Explanations for Their Confidence Ratings and What That Means for Calibration," *Learning and Instruction* 24 (2013): 4-14.

recognize that I have a lot to learn and should therefore approach theological conversations with humility and curiosity. That is not to say that I don't have some knowledge of the nature of God, or that I don't already have information that informs my perspective, but that I ought to approach it with openness. When someone approaches me to ask for an opinion, rather than offering a less-than-thoughtful response, especially if the topic is important or complicated, I ought to assess my confidence rating and use that to inform the language that I use and the posture I take in the conversation. It is likely that there are many times when I have more to learn than I have knowledge to share. *This posture of learning that embraces uncertainty will be a more accurate reflection of reality, which is a move toward righteousness.*

GOOD THINKING USES YOUR EMOTIONAL CUES

Major decisions should not be made quickly when someone is angry, grieving, lonely, hungry, tired, or all of those at once. Strong emotions are cues that we have a stake in the outcome. They should be used to help us inform decision-making, not impair decision-making. *Emotions are ways of getting our attention and should prompt us to pursue accuracy.* We are most tempted to lean into a self-positivity bias to feel better when we are feeling bad. As I mentioned in chapter two, my youngest daughter starting kindergarten triggered a lot of emotions for me. From my earliest memories, I knew that I wanted to be a mother. I planned my career around being able to be present and involved in all the important moments of my children's lives. For ten years before sending my youngest to kindergarten, I had a child under five who was spending a majority of their time with me. Combined, my three daughters spent two years in preschool; the rest of it was spent in our home and with a combination of parents and babysitters. Most semesters, I only taught classes on Tuesdays and Thursdays so that I could be home with them for the rest of the week. I had been dreading the day my youngest started kindergarten for years. Needless to say, but just to make it explicit, I am sad that these days with pre-schoolers at home are over. I am thankful for the time I spent with them, and thankful that I got to be the kind of parent I always wanted to be. At the retirement of my department chair, who made this schedule possible, I thanked her for allowing me to be the mom that I had always wanted to be.

A few days before my youngest daughter went to kindergarten, I was talking with a friend savoring the last days of summer, when she started talking about someone who made a choice to send her child to full-time daycare. Rather than slowing down my thinking, my emotions fueled a rush to judgment. "How could anyone choose to miss moments with their child that they will never get back?" My outrage at the decision was then followed by sadness that this person did not even realize the preciousness of what they were missing. These strong emotional responses eventually prompted me to consider why I reacted so strongly, but not before I expressed my judgment in a way that doesn't make me feel proud of myself now. My own experiences and the priming of my daughter going to kindergarten set me up to judge and justify my own choices. I wanted to be right. When I am thinking more accurately, I recognize and validate the complicated decisions that other parents make.

I share this anecdote not because I think emotions are inherently biasing, but *because they can set us up to pursue accuracy.* They alert us to situations that may be dangerous or in my case tied to strong values. I feel anger and sadness because I place a high value on time spent with my children. This is not wrong, but it doesn't have to be everyone else's value. I don't need to be offended by someone else's disagreement. My emotions help me to notice and evaluate my values. Emotions can move us from fast to slow thinking *if we recognize them as signals.* There are times when all of us experience an emotional re-action but realize that it might be heightened by sleep deprivation, so (hopefully) instead of giving in to a knee-jerk reaction, we go to sleep.

Imagine a close friend comes to you just weeks before his wedding. He starts to explain how anxious he is feeling about the impending commitment. Would you listen to the details of his story without probing deeper? Would you encourage him to ignore his feelings and get married? Assuming you are a good friend, this is not what you would do. Instead, this would be the beginning of a long conversation in order to better understand the cause of his feelings. You are motivated to help him to predict whether this marriage would end in divorce, so you are pursuing the most accurate information you can. You would access what you know about how data can predict divorce. The Gottman Institute has conducted research on how conversations that contain contempt, criticism, defensiveness, and stonewalling predict divorce.[19] Even in this seemingly subjective decision in which our culture suggests we "follow our hearts," there are ways to use and collect data to inform the decision. The feelings that accompany an impending wedding might be the result of real problems in a relationship that should not be ignored, or they could be the natural result of facing uncertainty. It is not possible to enter marriage with absolute certainty that you will be happy or stay together. It is a probabilistic judgment that is likely to include doubt, but it is *a decision that can be made righteously by trying to pursue accuracy.*

GOOD THINKING DISTINGUISHES BETWEEN FACTS AND OPINIONS

In the example from the previous section, where I judged someone based on their different parenting decisions, a logical response would be to point out that I was reacting to a difference in values or opinions, which should be treated differently from differences in knowledge and the interpretation of facts. Keith Stanovich, in his book *The Bias*

---

[19]Ellie Lisitsa, "The Four Horsemen: Criticism, Contempt, Defensiveness, and Stonewalling," The Gottman Institute, https://www.gottman.com/blog/the-four-horsemen-recognizing-criticism -contempt-defensiveness-and-stonewalling.

That Divides Us, makes the distinction between "belief bias" and "myside bias," and I agree that this separation is helpful.[20] Let me explain. In his terminology, "belief bias" is related to ideas that are testable. In this way, belief bias can be easily rectified through education and effortful thought. Given that "belief" is not currently defined this way, I think it might be simpler to think of this as "lack of facts bias" or an "ignorance-based bias." Stanovich distinguishes this from "myside bias" which he defines as an opinion that can be *based on* facts. This bias is harder to detect because it just looks like an opinion that might or might not be the result of an even-handed examination of all the relevant facts. Rather than calling this "myside bias," I think it might just be simpler to think of it as the bias that results from holding a strong opinion. He gives the example that "belief bias" would be that healthcare is the second largest budget item in the United States budget, but that the "myside bias" is that Americans spend too much money on healthcare. I think this distinction is important as we think about policing our own bias. If we are trying hard to pursue accuracy and avoid bias on an important topic about which we hold a strong opinion, *we need to be able to separate the bias that results from ignorance and the bias that results from filtering information through the lens of our opinion.* This is why Adam Grant recommends asking people to share the sources of their opinion as a way of understanding and approaching people with whom we disagree.[21] It is incredibly important in conversations, debates, and Twitter wars to understand the facts that underlie our opinions, but it might be less contentious and costly to our self-esteem and relationships if we engage in this thought process solo.

In one of the first experiments to test "myside bias," or the filtering of information through the lens of our deeply held beliefs, Norman

---

[20]Keith E. Stanovich, *The Bias That Divides Us: The Science and Politics of Myside Thinking* (Cambridge, MA: MIT Press, 2021), 4-9.
[21]Grant, *Think Again,* 147-50.

Feather had participants evaluate logic problems presented as informal arguments.[22] In a typical experiment, participants were told to accept as fact that "a charitable and tolerant attitude toward mankind helps to bring people together in love and harmony; and that Christianity always helps to bring people together in love and harmony." They were then told to evaluate the validity of the conclusion "Therefore a consequence of Christianity is a charitable and tolerant attitude toward mankind." Although this conclusion is not logically valid, highly religious participants had a harder time detecting the flaw in the logic than participants who were not highly religious. When we add the language of Christian faith to an argument, it can falsely elevate the conclusion beyond what is warranted. In many things, there ought to be ambivalence because all information is not available or fully comprehensible.

People believe many things that aren't true, mostly because they haven't done the work to examine the trustworthiness of the source. On the other hand, there are things that we choose to believe because they are useful even when we know the source is not reliable. Let's consider the use of personality tests. For the most part, the Big 5 personality test (extraversion, openness to new experiences, neuroticism, conscientiousness, agreeableness)[23] being the notable exception,[24] personality tests have little to no empirical evidence for their efficacy in predicting behavior, including job performance or the longevity of marriages—but those are two uses of them by people in power. The scientist in me recommends disposing with these altogether because they hide the real (and often uncomfortable) explanations for a person's behavior. On the other hand, people find them useful to put

---

[22]N. T. Feather, "A Structural Balance Model of Communication Effect," *Psychological Review* 71, no. 4 (1964): 291-313.

[23]Paul T. Costa and Robert R. McCrae, "Normal Personality Assessment in Clinical Practice: The NEO Personality Inventory," *Psychological Assessment* 4, no. 1 (1992): 5-13.

[24]Sampo V. Paunonen and Michael C. Ashton, "Big Five Factors and Facets and the Prediction of Behavior," *Journal of Personality and Social Psychology* 81, no. 3 (2001): 524-39.

language to behavior. I tell my students: personality tests are for entertainment. They help students think deeper about causes of behavior, but I am not sure the utility of giving language is sufficient to account for the lack of evidence and the way in which they exacerbate the fundamental attribution error.

The fundamental attribution error is the automatic tendency to assign an internal or dispositional explanation for a person's behavior while ignoring the potential situational explanation.[25] If someone trips, we assume they are clumsy without considering the slipperiness of the floor. If someone scores well on a test, we assume they are talented without considering the amount of effort that went into studying. If someone lies, we assume they are immoral without considering the consequences surrounding telling the truth. I tell students in my Intro to Psychology class that understanding the fundamental attribution error is one of the most important things I want them to take away from my class. This is why: we become too judgmental of a person's inner self based on way too little information, and that prevents us from seeing them clearly and loving them well. As I thought about becoming a parent, this was one of the things I wanted to teach my children to avoid. Recently, I saw that it might be working (at least a little bit). My middle daughter, in second grade, came home in a bad mood, and my initial probing suggested that her bad mood was from an irrational argument with her little sister. Later, I discovered that her bad mood was not about the argument with her sister and who owned the hand sanitizer, but about how she felt ignored at school.

I started asking her questions about why she felt ignored. I asked if anyone had said anything to her to make her feel as though she wasn't wanted. No. I asked her if her teacher had said anything to her about

---

[25]Douglas S. Krull et al., "The Fundamental Fundamental Attribution Error: Correspondence Bias in Individualist and Collectivist Cultures," *Personality and Social Psychology Bulletin* 25, no. 10 (1999): 1208-19.

this. No. So I told her that she is an awesome kid, and it was probably about something happening with the other kids and not something about her so she should think about another explanation for the kids ignoring her. I took a shower, and then she came back to me because she thought she had figured it out. The kids had recently changed seating arrangements, and at this new table, the other kids were leaning away from my daughter to talk to other kids. Their physical move away from her made her feel excluded. I told her it makes sense that it would feel bad. Then I suggested that it is possible that the kids at her table liked her but wanted to be able to talk during class, and knowing that she doesn't talk during class, chose to move closer to the kids who would be willing to misbehave. This explanation made sense to my daughter and to me. The kids don't dislike my daughter, but they do really like talking during class.

Now, I could have thought about my daughter's strong personality and concluded that there is something about my daughter that elicits this reaction from other kids, but it is much more likely that it is something about the rewards in the kids' environment that is the best explanation. Is it possible that personalities could be at play? Yes. The first reason personalities shouldn't be the default explanation is that research suggests behavior is more often predicted by environmental explanations.[26] The second reason is that changing personalities sounds impossible, but changing situations is feasible. The fundamental attribution error as the default explanation for behavior is probabilistically more likely to be wrong and more likely to feel unchangeable. Finally, reversing the fundamental attribution error feels a lot more like grace. We are not flawed, but our situations are complicated and strong contributors to our behavior. So, even though my suggestion of training people to reverse the fundamental attribution error will sometimes be wrong, it feels like a better bias. In situations

---

[26]Walter Mischel, *Personality and Assessment* (New York: Psychology Press, 2013).

of uncertainty, the outcomes of different beliefs need to be factored into the assessment. *In order to avoid both the fundamental attribution error and the myside bias, we need to pursue accuracy by questioning the quality of the facts that underlie our conclusions.*

DECONSTRUCTION AND RECONSTRUCTION

To close this chapter, I'm going to use the analogies of metaphorical construction, deconstruction, and housecleaning to explain how we can use the strategies of embracing doubt, thinking probabilistically, using your emotional cues, and evaluating the source of your conclusions to be rigorous in pursuing accuracy and righteousness. Even before I heard the term "deconstruction of faith,"[27] I have been interested in faith formation, and how students navigate faith after graduating from a Christian university. At the time when the term *emerging adults* was being established to explain the life stage after adolescence before taking on the responsibilities of adulthood, I was part of a research project that followed the trajectories of students graduating from three different evangelical universities. One of the major findings was that these "emerging adults" were not so much leaving the faith as they were leaving evangelical churches for more mainline denominations.[28] This struck me as a good thing at the time because it provided evidence that while at university, students reexamined faith and then chose to pursue faith in ways that deviated, but not dramatically, from the faith of their parents. This was data that was collected between 2007 and 2009. I don't have confidence that this is the story of today's emerging adults graduating from Christian universities, which leads me to the deconstruction process that might be a better description of what is happening for current graduates.

---

[27]David Newheiser, *Hope in a Secular Age: Deconstruction, Negative Theology, and the Future of Faith* (Cambridge: Cambridge University Press, 2022).

[28]E. Devers, "Emerging Adulthood and the Faith-Health Relationship: An Application of the Theory of Planned Behavior" (Paper, American Psychological Association annual meeting, San Diego, CA, August 2010).

I have a knee-jerk negative reaction to "deconstruction." The demolition of faith makes me feel sad because I have such a strong identity as a person of faith. If you have read the previous chapters in this book, you understand that I am arguing for having "child of God" and "sinner saved by grace" as the central identity. As I was talking with a former student about deconstruction, I realized that when I think of deconstruction of faith, I am imagining someone who has felt rejected by the church and then wants to tear it down in retaliation. Many of us have felt rejected by the church recently over a variety of issues. In response to rejection, it makes sense to take a wrecking ball and "deconstruct" or demolish the thing that has rejected you. I have felt this kind of rejection and have felt the urge to avoid church.

As my former student was talking, I realized that her picture of deconstruction is more like taking bricks of belief from a house and deciding whether the belief that the brick represents is really necessary to the house. Any brick that is not needed is then removed from the house. For example, for many people a belief in the literal creation story is important to their faith, but then after learning new information about the topic, they are forced to decide whether this brick is needed for faith to be maintained. A person can decide that it is necessary to know whether the Bible's creation story represents a literal or literary description in order for their faith to be true. Creating a house of faith based on accurate beliefs has been central to evangelicals. Therefore, it makes sense that evangelicals would be very motivated to deconstruct by examining each belief carefully and building a house of faith based on correct beliefs.

It seems entirely possible that many people believe they are deconstructing in the rational manner represented by the "brick-by-brick" version of the analogy but are actually behaving more in line with the "wrecking ball" version. We like to dress up our wrecking ball behaviors with rational stories, like the lawyer who wants to be right.

We don't want to admit that the reason we walked away from a set of beliefs was because our feelings were hurt, even though that explanation might be accurate. We would rather tell ourselves and others the story that we walked away from faith because after rational examination of the beliefs, the beliefs were not accurate. I think all of us should be carefully examining what belief bricks we use to build a worldview, like a scientist in search of accuracy.

Rather than using the deconstruction metaphor, let's use a house cleaning analogy, as if we are on an episode of *Hoarders*.[29] Instead of houses full of needless trash, we are in a house full of beliefs, and we are a person that hoards. I will admit to watching more of these episodes than a person should watch after realizing that they follow the same pattern. In the beginning, we see the house full of trash that is preventing a person from functioning. We meet the person's family members who see the dysfunction and want to help. Then we meet the person who hoards, who clearly has an attachment to objects. Psychologist Robert Abelson argues that beliefs are like possessions.[30] Some beliefs are useful, like the dishes in a person's house. When the hoarding experts come to help sort possessions, they let the person who struggles with hoarding keep the useful stuff. Other beliefs have more symbolic functions. They allow us to show others what groups we belong to and what our individual beliefs are. These are possessions that the organizing experts have a much harder time helping people get rid of. I have never seen an episode of this show where the person who hoards gets rid of all the nonfunctional stuff. Every episode involves the person who hoards having a breakdown over something that everyone else in their life wants them to get rid of but is very valuable to them.

To bring the analogy back to beliefs, if pure rationality were possible, we should only keep the functional and accurate beliefs. Only

---

[29]*Hoarders*, produced by George Butts (A+E Networks, 2009–2021).
[30]Robert P. Abelson, "Beliefs Are Like Possessions," *Journal for the Theory of Social Behaviour* 16, no. 3 (1986): 223–50.

beliefs that are rooted in a high degree of confidence in their accuracy should be kept. But imagine walking into a house devoid of all color and decoration, with only minimal furniture. These houses are rare. I almost didn't go on a third date with my husband when I saw the spartan conditions of his apartment and wardrobe. There are many beliefs that we use to decorate our lives that we don't have a high degree of confidence in, but they may make life better. For example, when our electricity went off, I decided to choose to believe the soonest estimate from the power company of when we would get power back rather than the latest estimate, because it made me feel better to believe the sooner one. Without any evidence to favor one estimate over the other and little confidence in either one, I chose to believe the one that made me happiest. We all have many beliefs for which we have little evidence.

What separates normal people from people who hoard? For people who hoard, the stuff in their house has created difficulties in their relationships and destroyed the integrity of their house. Most of them can no longer use the kitchen or bathroom, and at least one family member has stopped visiting them because of the hazardous conditions of their house. Now apply this hoarding analogy to beliefs. If your beliefs are wreaking havoc in your relationships, you might want to consider how important these beliefs are. If you can't carry on a conversation that ends in a hug, you might want to look more closely at your conversation topics. If your blood pressure is skyrocketing every time you read the news or talk to people you disagree with, you should question the significance you are placing on your beliefs. If I claim to be a follower of Jesus, who values love, I recommend questioning any belief that makes loving people harder.

Should we think about ourselves as those who are building or deconstructing? Are we acquiring new beliefs and possessions or are we decluttering? The answer is probably "both" to both questions. As I write this, I am thinking about a college freshman sitting in an introductory psychology class wondering what this class is about and why it should matter. As the student considers what to believe, the building, deconstruction, acquiring, and decluttering should involve consideration of what evidence supports those beliefs. I hope that psychology helps us understand what constitutes good evidence. We should try to build and acquire and keep the things that we have confidence in as quality material. We should be taking time to think rationally about the things that compose a worldview. I would also encourage you to hold on to some of the useful ideas that might not have the same level of rigorous evidence, but also to be willing to get rid of them pending disconfirming evidence. Discuss these ideas with your professors. As it relates specifically to issues of faith, I recommend that you take theology classes, read deep books, and join the important debates. You can engage in the "brick-by-brick" method. At the same time, practice spiritual disciplines of prayer, meditation, fasting, hospitality, forgiveness, humility, and Bible reading. These practices of faith set the mindset for all the other "brick evaluations." Spending time in prayer is what helps me to put the other debates in perspective in terms of their importance. Some of the questions I had earlier in my life I have abandoned (at least temporarily) as ones that are too difficult to answer, and even if I had confidence in the answer, I'm not sure how it would change my behavior. If I were to summarize where I now stand on the questions of deconstructing and decluttering beliefs, I would echo the words of Madeleine L'Engle, "I do not think that I will ever reach a stage when I say, 'This is what I believe. Finished.' What I believe is alive . . . and open to growth."[31] So set up good conditions for thinking by examining the accuracy of what fills the file folders (like the bricks of your house)—and keep building, because the process of pursuing accuracy is never over.

---

[31]Madeleine L'Engle, "Madeleine L'Engle," in *The Courage of Conviction: Prominent Contemporaries Discuss Their Beliefs and How They Put Them into Action*, ed. Phillip L. Berman (New York: Ballantine Books, 1986), 171.

CHAPTER FOUR SUMMARY

If you practice good slow thinking in pursuit of accuracy, it will eventually build better fast thoughts because good slow thinking will become habitual. One cue to good slow thinking is to consider your motives in situations because you will look to confirm what you want to believe. A second way to improve slow thinking is to assign probabilities or confidence ratings to decisions. These will help you more accurately assess future probabilities and prompt humility. Strong emotions are cues that slow thinking is needed in order to understand the source of the emotions. Evaluating the quality of the source of opinions and ideas is a hallmark of good slow thinking. Engaging in good slow thinking should result in a reevaluation of beliefs and opinions to be more accurate and righteous.

APPLICATION: UNBIASED NUDGES

- Acknowledge how your motivation is biasing your thinking. You want to take a vacation. You want to buy shoes on sale. You want to use confessions to catch bad guys.

- Acknowledge that all decisions include elements of uncertainty that contribute to doubt. Add confidence ratings to your opinions and decisions. Use those ratings to inform how you interact with others.

- Check your bias by examining causes of strong emotional reactions.

- Look for the cases where you have used personality as an explanation; consider the role of the situation instead.

- Engage in construction, deconstruction, and/or reorganization of your thoughts and beliefs. Consider each important belief. What is its origin? What is its purpose? How much confidence do I have in its accuracy? Does it bring me joy? Am I willing to discard it in the face of disconfirming evidence?

FIVE

LESS-BIASED FAST THINKING

IF MOST THINKING WERE SLOW THINKING, then the last chapter might have gone a long way to help us reduce bias in our thinking. Unfortunately, most of our thoughts are likely happening below awareness. Therefore, this chapter is dedicated to reducing bias in fast thinking, since this represents a majority of our thinking. As mentioned in chapter three, we have primary control over the things we are able to change; we have secondary control over our mindset. In each section of this chapter, I will describe environmental conditions that can affect bias and how pursuing accuracy can help us resist bias. The conditions are ways to set up our environments to improve our fast thinking. For some of us, some of the time, we will have primary control over our external environmental conditions. For some of us, the rest of the time, we don't have primary control over the environmental conditions and will have to use secondary control over our internal conditions (mindset) to reduce bias. For example, if I have the power to manipulate my mood by playing music, watching short videos, or meditating, I have primary control. Each of these things will impact fast thinking. On the other hand, there are times when I get in a funk, and moods are hard to change, so I must settle for a change in mindset, which may require more deliberate slow thinking.

GOOD THINKING IS AFFECTED BY MOOD

To be a less-biased fast thinker, start by considering how the things in the physical environment are impacting how you think. One of those environmental conditions is mood. You have probably had the experience of lashing out at a friend only to realize later that your mood might have been a bigger influence on your reaction than the rude comment made by your friend. Conversely, while in a good mood, you might have come up with a whole list of good ideas that don't look as good when you read them later when you aren't in such a good mood anymore. My very first published paper was the result of my first experiment in graduate school on the relationship between mood and creativity.[1] The experiment was designed to explain an effect that had already been established: positive mood facilitates creativity.[2] Our thinking changes based on conditions like mood and motivation. Whenever I sit down to write or problem-solve, I am reminded of this, and I try to boost my mood before I start. Positive mood is not, however, universally better for thinking. Other evidence that suggests a positive mood can lead to more superficial processing of new information; a negative mood leads to more critical thinking.[3] It depends on the goal of thinking. To generate lots of ideas, get positive. To narrow the choices and make the best decision, a negative mood might be better. The experiment I conducted was designed to find evidence that could explain why people in positive moods are more creative.

Let me begin by explaining the experiment. First, students came into the lab and were put in a cubicle, where they watched one of three possible series of movie clips. The title of the experiment they signed up for was "Rating Movies." If the participant was lucky, he or she was treated to rating some funny clips from *Pretty Woman* and *Mrs. Doubtfire*. If the participant was only a little bit lucky, he or she watched clips from documentaries, including one on the position of

[1]Edward R. Hirt, Erin E. Devers, and Sean M. McCrea, "I Want to Be Creative: Exploring the Role of Hedonic Contingency Theory in the Positive Mood-Cognitive Flexibility Link," *Journal of Personality and Social Psychology* 94, no. 2 (2008): 214-30.

[2]Leila T. Worth and Diane M. Mackie, "Cognitive Mediation of Positive Affect in Persuasion," *Social Cognition* 5, no. 1 (1987): 76-94.

[3]Herbert Bless et al., "Mood and Persuasion: A Cognitive Response Analysis," *Personality and Social Psychology Bulletin* 16, no. 2 (1990): 331-45.

the Earth in space. If the participant was unlucky, he or she had to watch what I consider to be the worst movie clips of all time, including one in which Meryl Streep has to choose which child to keep and which to surrender to the Nazis in the movie *Sophie's Choice*. (I have never watched the entire movie to this day and am still mildly traumatized by watching her choose one child to die over and over as part of this experiment.) Then as if that wasn't bad enough, the same participants were then subjected to a clip from a movie in which Mary Tyler Moore and her husband are discussing the dissolution of their marriage following the death of their son.

After the participants rated these movie clips, I would come in (blind to which movies they watched, praise God) with a candle that I had purchased from Bath & Body Works. It was the "Awake" aromatherapy candle, but I told participants a different story about the power of the candle. When I came in with it, if a participant was lucky enough to be in "mood freezing condition," he or she heard my story of how "researchers at the University of Michigan were interested in the cognitive effects of aromatherapy and that this particular aromatherapy has a mood-freezing effect such that whatever mood you are in right now, you are likely to remain in for a fixed period of time." Participants in the non-mood-freezing condition got a similar spiel about the researchers at U of M, but no mention of the mood-freezing effect. Then I placed the candle in the cubicle and loaded the cognitive task on the computer.

At this point, regardless of the condition, all participants were asked to list modes of transportation; no instructions were given regarding how many responses were needed or how long the participants should persist at the task. Once they were done, participants were debriefed, and I explained that the candle did not have a mood-freezing effect, and I asked if they had been suspicious. Only one participant admitted suspicion. This participant worked at Bath & Body Works and recognized the candle as the "Awake" candle.

Many of you may now be wondering what the whole purpose of the experiment was, and why I was willing to lie to people on a regular basis in the name of science. The answer to the first question is that the experiment was designed to test an explanation for why people in positive moods are more creative. We were predicting that people would be most creative in the positive mood condition when the candle did *not* have a mood-freezing effect. The reason for this prediction is that people in positive moods (those who just watched the *Pretty Woman* clip) have to be picky about what they do in order to maintain a positive mood, and since creativity maintains positive mood, they should be most likely to approach the task creatively in order to maintain their positive mood. Some of the most creative modes of transportation included answers like "literature," "email," or "LSD" as a mode of transportation. Many of these came from the positive mood/non-mood-freezing condition. Participants in neutral mood (bored from watching documentaries) and negative mood conditions didn't need to work hard to maintain mood; nearly anything would be an improvement; therefore, they didn't need to work hard to approach the task creatively. We were also making the prediction (and found the results to support) that those in the positive mood mood-freezing condition wouldn't need to be creative to maintain mood because they believed that the candle itself would maintain mood.

A major point of my first experiment is that we are hedonically motivated: we want to pursue pleasure and avoid pain, which sounds a lot like the general motivation of wanting to feel good about ourselves. This hedonic motivation also has important implications for thinking about bias. Turns out there are many conditions under which thinking is painful.[4] In one experiment, researchers demonstrated that when participants were left alone in a room for an extended period of time with nothing but a shocking device (which has

---

[4]Timothy D. Wilson et al., "Just Think: The Challenges of the Disengaged Mind," *Science* 345, no. 6192 (2014): 75-77.

already been established as pain inducing), 67 percent of men and 25 percent of women go ahead and shock themselves.[5] The researchers argue that solitude is painful even in small amounts. We have become so conditioned to constant entertainment that a few moments alone to think is uncomfortable.

On the other hand, personality differences are also at play when considering how people experience sitting alone with their thoughts. Some people have been identified as high in the need for cognition.[6] These people enjoy thinking and are much more likely to enjoy sitting in silence. The hedonic consequences of thinking are different for them. When I was a child, my mother bought me a book titled *The Way Things Work*.[7] In retrospect, I think she was tired of explaining things to me. The need for cognition is wonderful; it motivates good thinking. The downside of personality differences like high need for cognition is that using need for cognition as an explanation for behavior feels very fatalistic and reflective of a fixed mindset to assume we are either born with high need for cognition or not. It is not very comforting to think that the only people who will enjoy thinking are born with that desire. Fortunately, psychologists have found that there are situations that induce high need for cognition—specifically when the information is relevant to our lives.[8] When something is relevant to our survival or happiness, we are more motivated to think; the hedonic consequences have shifted such that even people who are typically low in need for cognition behave like the people who are high in need for cognition.

The idea that we think hard when information is relevant makes sense even if we are shallow, low-in-need-for-cognition thinkers (although, honestly, would any of them be reading this book?). If the

[5]Wilson et al., "Just Think."
[6]John T. Cacioppo and Richard E. Petty, "The Need for Cognition," *Journal of Personality and Social Psychology* 42, no. 1 (1982): 116-31.
[7]David Macaulay and Neil Ardley, *The Way Things Work* (Boston: Houghton Mifflin, 1988), 22-33.
[8]Cacioppo and Petty, "The Need for Cognition."

information is vital to life, we pay attention. The problem is sometimes we don't know what information is vitally important and what isn't. For educators to engage students in the kind of thinking required for learning, they have the challenge of figuring out how to increase the relevance of the material for students. If it's not possible to make information relevant, educators decide that they need to make learning fun. In this way, educators decide to try to change the hedonic consequences of thinking. On the surface this seems great, but like all things related to bias, it is not that simple. The data on positive-mood thinking is that it leads to shallow processing.[9] On the other hand, some of the best data in persuasion literature is on the role of comedy.[10] I would argue that it is in part due to the mix of positive emotion that then mixes with a negative or surprising message. The positive mood opens the door to listen and then the negative or surprising twist of the joke makes the point sink in deeper. Unfortunately, not every teaching experience can have the polish of a well-crafted comedy set.

If you want to pursue good fast thinking, consider how your mood contributes to your thinking. If you are wanting to think more creatively at the start of your day, consider how some positive mood boosters (like coffee or another favorite beverage) might be helping your unconscious mind start thinking more creatively. If you have become habituated to a beverage, maybe try music or pictures as positive mood primes. Mood manipulators are just small ways to direct your fast thinking that don't require much effort once they become part of your regular routine.

GOOD THINKING IS BASED IN HABITS

It *seems* as though good thinking and good behavior are both the result of willpower. More recent research suggests, however, that this

---

[9]Bless et al., "Mood and Persuasion."

[10]Lauren Feldman and Caty Borum Chattoo, "Comedy as a Route to Social Change: The Effects of Satire and News on Persuasion About Syrian Refugees," *Mass Communication and Society* 22, no. 3 (2018): 277-300.

kind of willpower doesn't exist.[11] This feels like a strong statement, and it probably is too strong—but doesn't it make you feel less judgmental toward yourself? It makes me feel better—now I feel less culpable for moral failings. *The data suggest that the ability to follow through with difficult behaviors over the long term is really about conditions and habits, not willpower.* As a side note, practicing gratitude can double your self-control.[12] Consider a regular gratitude practice as the habit that can springboard the development of other habits. Thinking about creating good habits and removing bad habits feels more solvable than getting more willpower. I am not a philosopher. I am a pragmatist. I want to be holy. I can't get there alone. I need Jesus. That is where most Christians stop. The problem I have is that I need to pray the prayer that says, "I have faith, forgive my unbelief." Belief is not enough to change habits. Faith without works is dead. If I want to glorify God, the obvious answer is to pray and practice spiritual disciplines such as gratitude. We do have the ability to exert primary control on most of our habits, we just need to tap into it.

If habit, instead of willpower, is the best predictor of moral behavior, as many economists, psychologists, and data suggest, this should be encouraging. Instead of having willpower to resist unhealthy food, I just need to develop a habit of eating healthy food, by making it easy to eat the healthy food (buying it at the store and keeping it on hand in my fridge) and hard to eat the unhealthy food (having to make a special trip out to get the food). The difficult part is that starting a habit might be hard. In terms of fast and slow thinking, habit is more like automatic fast thinking; it is just what we do, and we may not even remember why we do it. It is a matter of doing what is easiest in a particular environment. Willpower, on the other hand, is more like

---

[11]David T. Neal, Wendy Wood, and Aimee Drolet, "How Do People Adhere to Goals When Willpower Is Low? The Profits (and Pitfalls) of Strong Habits," *Journal of Personality and Social Psychology* 104, no. 6 (2013): 959-75.

[12]David DeSteno et al., "Gratitude: A Tool for Reducing Economic Impatience," *Psychological Science* 25, no. 6 (2014): 1262-67.

controlled slow thinking—difficult and draining. It involves resisting the temptation to do what is easiest in the environment. This is why studying on a bed is not a good idea. Self-control is like a muscle that can be exhausted with use;[13] thus, resistance should be saved for the really important work. Most people should harness habit and not will-power as an antidote to immorality.

When I was a graduate student, I believed strongly in willpower. Like most PhD students, I had to take qualifying exams after the end of the summer of my second year of graduate school. My exams consisted of two days in a room without internet to answer questions that I would not know in advance and that could be on any major topic in social psychology. To pass these exams, I needed to have memorized the content and citations of hundreds of articles and then be able to weave those together into coherent arguments in response to the questions. After the written portion of the exam, I would need to orally defend my written arguments in front of the social psych faculty. If I failed, I would not receive my PhD and would be done with graduate school. The stakes were especially high because at that point, I didn't have a back-up career plan.

I consulted the work on self-control, and specifically Baumeister's work arguing that self-control is a limited resource,[14] and decided that I would need to direct all my self-control toward studying and allow myself to lower my self-control in other areas of life. I gave myself permission to watch trashy reality TV and to eat whatever I wanted that summer. I could also drink as much coffee as I wanted. I have long given my willpower credit for passing my exams.

Looking back however, I realize that what I did, without realizing it, was not about exerting my willpower, but was the result of developing a habit. Every morning that summer I went to Barnes and Noble at a

---

[13]Mark Muraven and Roy F. Baumeister, "Self-Regulation and Depletion of Limited Resources: Does Self-Control Resemble a Muscle?," *Psychological Bulletin* 126, no. 2 (2000): 247-59.
[14]Muraven and Baumeister, "Self-Regulation and Depletion of Limited Resources."

particular time, ordered a refillable cup of coffee (chocolate truffle being my favorite) and sat down with printed copies of articles to study. Once I had completed a certain amount of studying, I allowed myself to browse books. I did this every day all summer. What habit researchers would notice in my description is that I built in rewards and pleasant experiences to reduce the need for more willpower. It is not as hard to study if I have my favorite coffee. It becomes less hard to go to Barnes and Noble to study if that is what I had done for the past three days.

I was listening to Wendy Wood, a habit researcher, talking about her running habit on a podcast.[15] Like many people, before having kids, she made time to exercise. After having kids, there was never a convenient time to do it, so the habit died. As she was considering how to bring the habit back, she realized that she had to reduce the costs and barriers to running. So she decided to start sleeping in her exercise clothes, so that she would have one less thing to do in the morning before running. She also had entertaining material prepared to listen to. She changed the incentive structure of exercise.

Even with behaviors that I know are rewarding to me, such as writing this book, it is in my best interest not to rely solely on will, but to instead develop a habit of writing. During the week, I write immediately after taking the girls to school, and then the rest of the day I feel the joy of having already written something, and I get the mood boost that comes from creativity in the first place. Given that this benefit exists, I know I should also write on Saturdays, but the other feature of the routine (dropping the girls off at school) is missing. It takes a little bit of extra willpower, but I do a few of the other pieces of the routine, like making coffee and emptying the dishwasher and sitting down with my computer in the same place at the same time. The more similar it is to routine, the more my mind can *rely on the automatic thinking of habit and reduce the effort of the controlled thinking of willpower.*

---

[15]Shankar Vedantam, "Creatures of Habit," December 30, 2019, in *Hidden Brain*, NPR, podcast, https://hiddenbrain.org/podcast/creatures-of-habit.

GOOD THINKING HAPPENS WHEN
OTHERS ARE THINKING WELL

Surrounding yourself with other good thinkers is a second environmental condition over which you might be able to exert primary control. A few months ago, a fellow psych prof in my department asked me if I believed that people could change. He had heard students talking about my class, and one of the messages they had received was that I don't believe people can change. Bless his heart, my fellow psych prof who specializes in counseling wanted to make sure that I didn't really believe that, because what a discouraging thing that would be for someone to believe that people can't change. At first, I gave him a perplexed look, because in my mind I never said that people can't change and especially not to students in a class. Then upon further reflection, I realized that the message students were getting was that

1. there are automatic thought processes that happen below awareness;
2. these thoughts are influenced by environment and culture;
3. no single person changes culture;
4. therefore, we are chained to our faulty automatic thoughts without any hope for change.

Those students were paying attention.

On the other hand, I do believe people can change. As mentioned in the previous chapter, priming research leads to the conclusion that behavior is determined by the environment; thus, humans have very little control over behavior. At a conference, someone challenged the idea that humans have no control because they are behaving based on automatic thoughts, and John Bargh,[16] pioneering priming researcher, very graciously admitted that his thinking on the topic had changed since his writing of the strongly titled "Four Horsemen of

---

[16]J. Bargh, "How Real and Imagined Physical Experiences Influence Social Judgment and Behavior" (Invited Address, Midwestern Psychological Association, Chicago, May 2, 2014).

Automaticity" article.[17] He then referenced a dolphin screensaver that had been playing on the screen before his talk started and told the audience that the screensaver was an analogy for how he now thinks about behavior. Like dolphins swimming in the water, he argued that what happens under the water (automatic thoughts) influences what happens above the water (controlled thoughts) and that they both influence behavior.

So far, I have tried to make the case that fast (automatic) thoughts are present in bias and that controlled thinking can help reduce the impact of the bias. This is markedly easier to accomplish in an environment where other people are also using controlled thinking to correct bias. When I started graduate school, in addition to being shaped by my first time conducting an experiment, I was shaped by entering a new culture. The culture I came from was nice. Very nice. We gave each other encouragement with very little criticism. This was true academically and socially and is what I consider one of the hallmarks of the undergraduate Christian college subculture that shaped me. My graduate school advisor is one of my favorite people. When we met, his office was covered in his children's art, and he was (still is) perpetually smiling. Imagine my surprise when we met to go over the first draft of a grant I was writing, and he had nothing but criticism to give me. I was shocked and my feelings were hurt (fortunately, I had the wisdom to hide my feelings). It didn't take me too long to figure out that I had entered a new culture, where people liked me personally *and* gave me a lot of critical feedback on my work. One could even argue that *because* they liked me, they gave me a lot of critical feedback on my work. I became a better writer, thinker, and person because of it.

Simultaneously, I was getting involved in a new Christian culture where we called each other out on sinful behavior. The environment

---

[17]J. Bargh, "The Four Horsemen of Automaticity: Awareness, Efficiency, Intentions and Control," in *Handbook of Social Cognition*, vol. 1, ed. Thomas K. Srull and Robert S. Wyer, 2nd ed. (Hillsdale, NJ: Lawrence Erlbaum, 1994), 1-40.

wasn't as nice as I was used to in my previous Christian college sub-culture. I was challenged to recognize that I had relied on an automatic bias that equated niceness with kindness. I needed to learn the difference. I needed people in my life who weren't as concerned with my feelings as they were with the truth. This culture of love and truth-telling promotes good thinking.

There is a likely second reason that students think I believe people can't change. When I teach about cognitive dissonance, which is the uncomfortable internal conflict we feel when our behavior and beliefs don't match, I present them with scenarios. Imagine you do something immoral—you "borrow" something from a roommate without asking. You hide the truth from someone you love so as not to hurt their feelings. It is very unlikely that you will reflect on that behavior, feel bad about it, and change your behavior. Instead, you will change your thoughts about stealing and lying, adjusting them to be more lenient to justify your behavior, just like my student changed her definition of sex to make her behavior fit. Behavior change requires a big dose of dissonance, and because behavior change is harder than attitude change, attitude change prevails most frequently. If you are a student listening closely, the bottom line is, people rarely change.

If this is depressing, which it is, I'm going to offer an alternative idea. Implicit thoughts are hard to change without a cultural change. Dissonance can't change behavior without a large dose, which no one really wants. So instead of trying to change hearts and minds, why not take a lesson from the behaviorists and encourage behavior change without attitudes? Let me try to explain. Like the recommendations on habit formation, we need to set up the environments to change behaviors and stop trying to change hearts and minds. I love the work of Phillip Atiba Solomon, who works with police through the Center for Policing Equity.[18] He uses the police's own statistics to

---

[18]Philip Atiba Solomon, "How We Can Make Racism a Solvable Problem—and Improve Policing," TED, April 2019, www.ted.com/talks/dr_phillip_atiba_goff_how_we_can_make_racism_a _solvable_problem_and_improve_policing.

address where there are problems, and then comes in to figure out the problem. He is not trying to change the hearts and minds of police officers. If the problem is that police officers make worse (more biased) decisions when in a foot chase, he advises to change the protocols surrounding foot chases. Don't call police officers racists and offer superficial (non-effective) attitude training. All of us want to fix problems, so let's change the environment to change behaviors by *creating cultures of good thinking*. Given changes in the environment, people change.

GOOD THINKING HAPPENS WHEN NEEDS ARE MET

Most of us are already doing what we can to avoid scarcity. We want to make sure we have enough food, friends, money, and time to build a good life. As much as is possible, *your thinking will benefit from setting up your environment to remind you of abundance instead of scarcity.*[19] When hungry, the scarcity of food can make it hard to think about anything other than food, a situation that supports the idea that people behave worse when they are "hangry." Scarcity can show up in many forms, including a scarcity of civility. Imagine being cut off in traffic or being on the receiving end of a rude comment on social media. Rudeness hijacks slow thinking, even when we don't think it bothers us.[20] Our brains get short circuited, and we go into fight or flight. The ability to make thoughtful decisions becomes more difficult. On the one hand, this is like any other cognitive load (cognitive load is what dominates our thinking). Under load conditions, automatic thinking prevails because the resources aren't there for slow thinking. The same thing happens under conditions of rudeness. Think of the last time you were on the receiving end of someone's rude behavior. It becomes harder to think clearly, and your body responds—

---

[19]John Voorheis, Nolan McCarty, and Boris Shor, *Unequal Incomes, Ideology and Gridlock: How Rising Inequality Increases Political Polarization* (Rochester, NY: SSRN, 2015).

[20]Shankar Vedantam, "How Rude!," April 11, 2022, in *Hidden Brain*, NPR, podcast, https://hiddenbrain.org/podcast/how-rude.

your heart rate increases. Hearing what the other person is saying becomes harder and harder because you are responding to the attitude instead of the words.

Being on the receiving end of rudeness is the most powerful dose of the scarcity of civility, but just witnessing rudeness is enough to reduce the ability to think clearly. As I think about what nurses have faced over the past few years, I can't help but think of the human cost of rudeness. When nurses, police, and other first responders are in life and death situations, we need them to be able to think slowly with all their cognitive resources at their disposal. By adding load to an already stressful situation, mistakes become more likely.

Like experiencing rudeness, experiencing other forms of scarcity changes the cognitive resource load.[21] Scarcity focuses thinking on what is lacking. Results of a starvation experiment designed to help figure out how to best reintroduce food to Holocaust survivors found that participants were focused on food to the exclusion of all else. For example, when going to movies, these starving participants could recall in great deal what the main characters ate during the movie but had poor memory for the movie's plot. While most of us have not experienced starvation, many of us have experienced the focused attention on what we most need—money, food, attention, and so on. Scarcity sharpens our attention on what is lacking but causes us to miss what is right in front of us. Most introductory psychology students have watched the video of the gorilla experiment.[22] Before watching the video, participants are instructed to count how many times a basketball is passed between players. In the middle of the experiment, a gorilla walks across the basketball court. Most participants, even radiologists trained to detect abnormalities, fail to see the

---

[21]Sendhil Mullainathan and Eldar Shafir, *Scarcity: Why Having Too Little Means So Much* (New York: Times Books, 2013).

[22]Trafton Drew, Melissa L.-H. Võ, and Jeremy M. Wolfe, "The Invisible Gorilla Strikes Again: Sustained Inattentional Blindness in Expert Observers," *Psychological Science* 24, no. 9 (2013): 1848-53.

gorilla because they are so focused on counting basketball passes. Scarcity does the same thing. We can't see the gorilla because we are focused on when and what we will eat.

People also experience scarcity mindset when they are reminded that other people are financially better off. The scarcity mindset that results from thinking about how other people have more reduces cognitive resources and results in worse decision-making. When people get on planes that require coach passengers to pass through the first-class section before taking their seats, there are higher numbers of confrontational incidents.[23] Not only does the income inequality difference manifest itself in the increased hostility on flights where coach passengers have to pass through first class, but homicide rates are higher in wealthy countries that have higher rates of income inequality, compared to wealthy countries with lower rates of inequality.[24]

It would be ideal to reduce this bias by never experiencing scarcity, but as most economists tell us, scarcity is everywhere. We are all experiencing scarcity of time and resources and are forced to make trade-offs. While that is true, scarcity is not always the thing that is occupying our cognitive resources, so it may be better to characterize this as extreme scarcity. I'm not foolish enough to think that some mindset shifts can eliminate extreme scarcity, but I do think *setting up environments that prime practicing abundance thinking can help combat misperceived scarcity.*

During the early days of the Covid-19 pandemic, I was outside pushing my kids on our playset while listening to the *Frozen II* soundtrack. For those of you who are intimately familiar with the *Frozen II* soundtrack, you will recognize the song, "Some Things

---

[23]Katherine A. DeCelles and Michael I. Norton, "Physical and Situational Inequality on Airplanes Predicts Air Rage," *Proceedings of the National Academy of Sciences* 113, no. 20 (2016): 5588-91.

[24]Roy Kwon and Joseph F. Cabrera, "Income Inequality and Mass Shootings in the United States," BMC Public Health 19, no. 1 (2019), 1-8.

Never Change."[25] I was listening to this song in a scarcity mindset, thinking about how much has changed (and not for the better), and one of the lines said, "We'll always live in a kingdom of plenty that stands for the good and the many." As I thought about that line and how in one sense, it is easy to look around a say, it's not a kingdom of plenty when people are literally starving. I could, however, think about that line and be reminded of the kingdom of God, how that kingdom is a kingdom of plenty that I can always live in, and that the kingdom is available to "the many." Christians ought to recognize that we have already received abundance we ought to be sharing with others. Christ came so that we could have abundant life. Security of identity is abundance. A secure identity as children of God and sinners saved by grace should give Christians the ability to be slower thinkers who are more generous.

GOOD THINKING HAPPENS WITH A BROADER PERSPECTIVE

If you are trying to set up conditions for good thinking, consider your mood, invite over some good thinkers from your social network, arrange your environment to make good behaviors easy, set up some reminders of abundance, and then look at the stars. For some of us, good thinking is hard because our thoughts are more like negative chatter than a productive conversation. Ethan Kross, a prominent psychologist, researches ways to harness our inner chatter.[26] He suggests that we need to broaden our perspective. The further out we get, the more we view others as part of a larger "us." Space travel increases a love for humanity and shifts the ratings of the severity of a problem.[27] I love this research. When I am feeling depressed about something that

[25]Kristen Anderson-Lopez and Robert Lopez, "Some Things Never Change," performed by Kristen Bell, Josh Gad, Jonathan Groff, and Idina Menzel, on *Frozen II Original Motion Picture Soundtrack*, Walt Disney, 2019.

[26]Ethan Kross and Gretchen Rubin, *Chatter: The Voice in Our Head, Why It Matters, and How to Harness It* (New York: Crown, 2022), 48-55.

[27]David B. Yaden et al., "The Overview Effect: Awe and Self-Transcendent Experience in Space Flight," *Psychology of Consciousness: Theory, Research, and Practice* 3, no. 1 (2016): 1-11.

I know is small but feels big, I am reminded that I need to *step back, see the bigger world, and put my problem in context*. We say things like "first-world problem." Sometimes saying this works well for me. It's a bit like the perspective-taking exercise of recognizing the moral distance between God and me and the moral distance between others and me. These are ways of broadening the perspective.

I want to look more closely at these perspective-shifting experiments in the hopes of drawing some wisdom. Perspective-shifting experiments focus on the experience of awe, which is defined as "the feeling we get in the presence of something vast that challenges our understanding of the world." Surveys of astronauts have shown that the experience of flight increases their appreciation for the earth, can elicit awe and gratitude, and increases a sense of social cohesion. These experiences motivate former astronauts to engage in political action for environmental causes and demonstrate a reduction in prejudice. Looking at the big view, literally from space, can motivate change, and shifts action away from small personal problems. Actor William Shatner went to space and experienced the same thing that astronauts have described previously, and he also eloquently described the experience of grief that accompanies witnessing the fragility of Earth. "It's a little tiny rock with an onion skin air around it. That's how fragile it all is. It's so fragile. We hang by a thread. . . . We're just dangling."[28] Witnessing fragility and brevity brings grief, and so it's not surprising that the oldest person to ever go to space might experience a large dose of perspective shifting, feel grief, and be motivated to write an entire book dedicated to his great-granddaughter about the experience.

Taking on a broader perspective can be helpful, and Ethan Kross suggests that even though not all of us will go to space, we can use

---

[28]Enrique Rivera, "William Shatner Experienced Profound Grief in Space. It Was the 'Overview Effect,'" NPR News, October 23, 2022, www.npr.org/2022/10/23/1130482740/william-shatner -jeff-bezos-space-travel-overview-effect.

small interventions to get a bigger perspective. One way is to address yourself in the second person, the way you would treat yourself if you were a friend to yourself instead of you. Another way is to broaden the time frame and ask whether you will be concerned about this issue a week from now, a month from now, or a year from now. It is also helpful to consider how the things you were concerned about in your past are not the things you are concerned about now. This is what I think of as the "this too shall pass" strategy. This has been infinitely helpful to me when my emotions are telling me I should make a major change to address a problem, and then I recognize that it is very likely that this problem will change on its own in a year, but I have no idea what problems making a major life change will create. Accepting that things won't be perfect for a period of time but knowing that "this too shall pass" has been great for my mental health. Experiencing awe is yet another way to broaden our perspective and quiet our inner chatter. Seeing the bigness of things and our relative smallness helps us see our ruminating thoughts differently.

Inducing awe is one of the best ways to broaden perspective, because experiencing something vast is part of the definition of awe. Awe increases prosocial behavior, and most relevant to this book, it diminishes the sense of self—such that people are more likely to categorize the self in universal categories,[29] like as a human or child of God after an experience of awe. Additionally, it reduces a need for cognitive closure, which means that awe facilitates slow thinking and may be an antidote to experiencing rudeness. Awe even increases an interest in science and increases the possibility of scientific discovery. All these positive effects of awe, especially in reducing bias, raise the question of how awe can be induced. Vastness and sanctity are features of awe. Researchers try to induce these feelings using virtual

---

[29]Paul K. Piff et al., "Awe, the Small Self, and Prosocial Behavior," *Journal of Personality and Social Psychology* 108, no. 6 (2015): 883–99.

reality, but given the important consequences of awe, it is worth pursuing as a practice through regular exposure to vastness and sanctity. Awe is linked to openness to new experiences, which is a personality trait. Instead of thinking about it that way, I would argue that just pursuing new experiences might link to awe, whether or not that is part of our personality.

Putting these pieces together challenges me to make a more concerted effort to pursue new experiences, especially where there is a component of vastness and sanctity. The simplest intervention to promote awe is to think about God's vastness. Spirituality is positively correlated with awe. When I was a graduate student, an agnostic professor of mine said, "When I look at the ocean, I think there is a God." Taking a moment daily to think about the vastness of God is one of the best ways to reduce bias. I am reminded of a favorite hymn, "How deep the father's love for us, how vast beyond all measure, that he should give his only son to make a wretch his treasure."[30] The other words that come to mind are from the hymn "The Love of God": "Could we with ink the ocean fill, and were the sky of parchment made, were every stalk on earth a quill, and every man a scribe by trade, to write the love of God above, would drain the ocean dry, nor could the scroll contain the whole, though stretched from sky to sky."[31] Vastness and sanctity are ingredients of awe that we can experience in songs and thoughts. Awe can provide salve to our souls after rudeness and have the added benefit of scientific discovery.

Open a window, get outside, recognize God's presence in people. Look at the stars. Go to a new place, try a new food, meet up with an old friend. Put up pictures of the ocean and the mountains. Contemplate the intricacy of a baby's foot. *Set up your environment to direct your attention toward the awe-inspiring things.* Give God the glory.

---

[30]Stuart Townend, "How Deep the Father's Love," track 9 on *Say the Word* (Kingsway Music, 1997).
[31]Frederick M. Lehman, "The Love of God," 1917.

CLEANING OUT THE CLOSET

Once you have set up conditions for good thinking, you should *conduct an audit of your environments*, including your closet. If you think about your physical closet and all the books and shows that focus on the topic of organizing your life, you might get inspired to get rid of a few things, but generally we are loss averse. We hate getting rid of things, and the things we have collected are things that we place more value on than other people do. Even superficial things like mugs become more valuable to us after we own them than they were before, which is called the endowment effect.[32]

The endowment effect has been studied in lots of contexts and was never more pronounced to me than when I walked around my in-law's home as the next curator of the memories attached to my mother-in-law's objects. These objects are very valuable to her, so much so that she wants to make sure her sons don't just give everything to Goodwill after her death. She has good reason to believe this is what would happen. She told me the stories of her mother's things (a woman I never met), the photos of old family farms, books that were written in German that came over when family members immigrated. I listened to these stories realizing that endowment is so strong that it spans generations, such that even though I had never met these people, and I married into this family, getting rid of their things feels wrong. My mother-in-law knows about the endowment effect implicitly, which is why she asked me to spend a day looking over these objects. The endowment effect is part of the reason that people hate cleaning closets and why it takes effort on the part of cleaning gurus to help us do it. I know I take a perverse interest in watching experts try to convince people who hoard to get rid of their stuff, sometimes including what is clearly trash to everyone except the person who struggles with hoarding.

[32]Daniel Kahneman, Jack L. Knetsch, and Richard H. Thaler, "Experimental Tests of the Endowment Effect and the Coase Theorem," *Journal of Political Economy* 98, no. 6 (1990): 1325-48.

I realize that suggesting that we clean out physical closets to improve thinking is not something most people want to do. I regularly read articles that promise we can have the most functional wardrobe with just these twenty pieces. I live in the Midwest and just weather alone makes me skeptical that this is possible for me. I have tried variations on this idea by picking out eight outfits for work in my closet so that I wouldn't have to think about what to wear in the morning. I also pared down my shoes to just four pairs (or five, counting flip flops). Paring down my shoes reduced the number of outfits that could be worn with them and thus simplified the whole dressing process all winter long to only wearing dresses that looked ok with knee-high leather boots to work. Decision fatigue is real, and since fatigue fatigue is also real, I didn't need to add decision fatigue to the mix. If you are feeling decision fatigue, you could start by auditing your closet so you spend less time choosing clothes.

There is value to subtraction. Marie Kondo understood from an early age that while getting rid of things is painful, if we are thinking about adding joy, then subtraction is beneficial. Lawmakers need to prune laws, gardeners need to prune plants, and we need to prune what we are willing to give our cognitive energy toward.[33] Marie Kondo's advice is to keep objects that spark joy, so if we follow the analogy, we should set up our houses, offices, and closets in ways that spark joy.[34] Now, even if it were possible that every object could bring joy, I don't think keeping everything would be entirely beneficial. Most of my environment is functional rather than joyful, but perhaps I could appreciate the function, and that appreciation is joyful. So, at the end of a good closet cleaning, everything ought to be more functional and more beautiful—clothes to fit different weather patterns and fewer clothes that are unflattering or infrequently worn.

---

[33]Leidy Klotz, *Subtract: The Untapped Science of Less* (New York: Flatiron Books, 2022).
[34]Marie Kondo, *The Life-Changing Magic of Tidying: A Simple, Effective Way to Banish Clutter Forever*, trans. Cathy Hirano (Toronto: Vermilion, 2014).

After reducing the things that are competing for space in your physical closet, it is time to consider how environments could be connected to our thought patterns. Are there places in our environment that help us experience awe? My dining room has big windows overlooking a ravine with a creek at the bottom. When I look out those windows, I notice the change in seasons, and I often feel like a smaller part of a bigger story that is going on out my windows. If you don't have a beautiful view, put something in a prominent place in your environment that represents awe to you. Also consider the pictures, messages, and colors that are around you. After an argument with my husband, I decided to take three of our wedding photos that had been on a shelf in the basement closet and prominently display them on our fireplace mantel. Underneath those three pictures, I literally balanced pictures of each of our three daughters. To me this represents that we have had happy times, we will have more happy times in the future, and that we are dependent on each other.

Set up your physical space with reminders of your important values. You may indeed need to keep a few of those reminders of dead relatives from your mother-in-law because they connect you to the value of honoring family. Your environment ought to reflect that you are a child of God, sinner saved by grace, who is participating in the work God has given you to do. You should be motivated when you enter your physical spaces to pick out file folders that are true and that promote righteousness. You should give easy access to thoughts that remind you of your position relative to God and relative to others.

CHAPTER FIVE SUMMARY

We need to make our fast thinking more accurate. Positive moods increase creative thinking; negative moods promote critical thinking. Use your moods to impact your thinking. Members of your social network influence your thinking; spend time with good thinkers. Your habits are reflections of your fast thinking so set up your environment to make it easier to build good habits. Avoid scarcity, and set up some reminders of abundance so scarcity doesn't control your thinking. Set up awe-primes in your environment to right-size your thinking. Fast thinking becomes better when it reflects important values; setting up your environment to prime your important values will improve your fast thinking.

APPLICATION: UNBIASED NUDGES

- Consider what mood would best facilitate the type of thinking you are trying to do and then manipulate your mood with music or movie clips.

- Think of the hard but good things you want to be doing. Remove the barriers that make it harder for you to want to do them. Add incentives to encourage the habit.

- Think about how you could add behaviors to your immediate culture that would make people feel both loved and open to critical feedback on their work and behavior.

- Reflect on the abundance you are currently experiencing.

- Manipulate awe by trying something new or going somewhere new, playing awe-inducing music, looking at pictures taken from space, or reflecting on the nature of God.

- Clean out your closet. Do an audit of the things you spend the most time thinking about. Consider your important values. Make sure your environments match your values.

SIX

REDUCING BIAS IN HOW YOU LOVE YOUR NEIGHBOR

INSTEAD OF JUST ENDORSING THEORIES, good psychological research and good books ought to lead to practical applications. Thus far, I have argued that our pursuit of accuracy ought to cause us to think about ourselves differently as well as how to develop better thought patterns, but the application of these principles to actual situations may have been hard to imagine. This chapter addresses three important realms of social decision-making (attribution, altruism, and attraction) and attempts to use the conditions and strategies from chapters four and five to make recommendations. Specifically, if we are leaning into our identities as children of God and are properly positioned to God and others, we can pursue accuracy because we don't need to use our motivation to maintain self-esteem to guide our opening of file folders. We should pursue accuracy with a spirit of intellectual humility, recognizing that we are sinners saved by grace. This pursuit of accuracy will have implications for *how we judge others, when we help others, and how we connect with others.* Starting from a recognition of our position relative to God and others will help us love our neighbors better.

My heart was grieved, just like millions of us were, when nineteen fourth graders and two teachers were gunned down in Uvalde, in part because the counterfactuals in that case were so strong. The counterfactuals (if onlys)[1] have always been strong in school shootings and in tragedies throughout time: If only someone had gone in sooner. If only the doors had been locked. Wanting to pursue righteousness prompts us generate counterfactuals so we can figure out how to stop future tragedies. We all want to figure out how to prevent more horror, so our natural thinking pattern after a tragedy is to consider what we could have done to stop it. So we play the "if only this . . . , then the outcome could have been different." A benefit can come from this kind of thinking, especially if people are easily able to identify and correct the problem. When suicide researchers figured out that just making the barriers on bridges higher would reduce suicide, they reduced suicides.[2]

In the case of the Uvalde school shooting, the counterfactuals were so strong because the response was so poorly handled by the police. It was reported that there were kids who bled out who might have been saved had the police responded sooner. Since the police were standing outside the school for an hour during the shooting, sooner feels very possible.[3] For those parents who were outside the school begging the police to intervene sooner, the counterfactuals were heartbreaking: "If only I would have ignored the police and gone in anyway," or "If only I could have said or done something to convince them to go in sooner." All the "If onlys." There are so many factors that might have made a difference, and they are so easy to imagine.

Upward counterfactuals, the kind of counterfactuals in which we imagine how things could have been better, are so emotional because they are tied to regret. When I first started reading the research on suicide, one of the things that surprised me was how most people who

[1] Neal J. Roese, "Counterfactual Thinking," *Psychological Bulletin* 121, no. 1 (1997): 133-48.
[2] Mike Pesca, "In Suicide Prevention, It's Method, Not Madness," July 8, 2008, in *The Bryant Park Project*, NPR, podcast, www.npr.org/templates/story/story.php?storyId=92319314.
[3] John Schuppe et al., "Police Waited for an Hour for Backup in the Uvalde Shooting. That's an Outdated Tactic, Experts Say," May 26, 2022, NBC News, www.nbcnews.com/news/us-news/uvalde-shooting-police-waited-hour-backup-rcna30622.

attempt suicide are relieved that it wasn't successful, and that most suicides are a split-second decision rather than a plan. Interviews with survivors reveal that only 13 percent reported thinking about the suicide for eight hours or longer; 70 percent for less than an hour, and 24 percent report less than five minutes of thinking preceded the attempt.[4] Given this, suicide prevention doesn't have to cure depression or suicidal ideation; it just has to slow down easy ways to die by suicide, such as bridge barriers and limiting easy access to firearms. At first glance, it seems like anyone who would consider jumping over a bridge, when confronted with a tall barrier, could just walk into traffic, but that is not what the data suggests. The more likely explanation is that the barrier slows down the person's thinking enough to lead them to reconsider the decision. The classic example is when England changed from coal gas (which can lead to asphyxiation) to natural gas in ovens. The suicide rate fell 30 percent. Removing the easy route to suicide from the kitchen reduced the number of suicides.

Data like this encourages my middle-of-the-night counterfactual thinking about the Uvalde school shooting because it makes me think that there might be small ways to slow down a process that could dramatically change the outcome. Automatic thinking could be at work, and a disruption might give controlled thinking a chance to change the direction of the decision. So first, it makes sense to set up conditions for good thinking to address the problem of mass shootings. The environment would need to make thinking easier by removing distractions, including others who are committed to a culture of good thinking, removing scarcity by providing for participants' physical and social needs, and providing opportunities to think more broadly by using pictures of space or other manipulations of awe. The thinkers would need to acknowledge their own bias, embrace doubt, practice intellectual humility, assign probabilities to proposed solutions, and

---

[4] Pesca, "In Suicide Prevention, It's Method, Not Madness."

evaluate the quality of the information that informs their opinion. This may look like the work of a think-tank or center. For the most part, we aren't being asked to solve problems like mass shootings, but we are trying to love our neighbors. Instead, let's think about how we can apply a similar process to *make our attributions more accurate and generous, increase helping, and facilitate attraction.*

ASSUME PEOPLE ARE LIKE YOU WHEN YOU MAKE ATTRIBUTIONS

If we have thought about our position relative to God and others and are pursuing accuracy, we should be thinking about our moral similarity to others, even and especially our neighbors. This is like getting an extra dose of humility, and it will reduce bias. Specifically, such thinking should cause us to *pursue accuracy by considering the way a person's situation impacts behavior* when we are trying to assign a cause to the behavior. Greg Lukianoff and Jonathan Haidt, in their book *The Coddling of the American Mind*, tell the story of a Latina student at Claremont McKenna College named Olivia.[5] Olivia wrote about her feelings of marginalization on campus in a student publication. In her essay, she described how other Latinos were more likely to be working as janitors or gardeners than as administrators or other professionals. She sent a copy of her essay to the dean of students, who replied to Olivia two days later. The dean wrote:

> Olivia—
>
> Thank you for writing and sharing this article with me. We have a lot to do as a college and community. Would you be willing to talk with me sometime about these issues? They are important to me and the (dean of students) staff and we are working on how we can better serve students, especially those who don't fit our CMC mold.

---

[5]Greg Lukianoff and Jonathan Haidt, *The Coddling of the American Mind: How Good Intentions and Bad Ideas Are Setting Up a Generation for Failure* (New York: Penguin, 2019), 53-57. Olivia was the name used in *The Coddling of the American Mind* and not her actual name.

I would love to talk with you more.

Best,

Dean Spellman[6]

As you read this email, consider how Olivia might have interpreted it. She could have seen this as evidence that the dean wanted to try and address her concerns. Instead, Olivia was offended by the dean's use of the word *mold*. Olivia posted the email to her Facebook page, adding, "I just don't fit that wonderful CMC mold! Feel free to share." The result of her post was a campus-wide protest with calls for Dean Spellman to resign. Dean Spellman apologized for the wording of the email, but the protests did not subside. Eventually, in response to the mounting pressure from students, social media, and national news coverage, Dean Spellman resigned.

There could have been a more productive outcome (addressing Olivia's concern regarding representation) had Olivia's response to the email been more generous. Instead of judging the dean's intention as racist or purposely exclusionary, Olivia could have assumed that she and the dean were both people who were trying to improve the culture of the university. Lukianoff and Haidt argue that our culture, and university culture in particular, has fostered the idea that "life is a battle between good people and evil people, and if you disagree with us, you're one of the evil people."[7] Conversations are different when both parties assume the other is also one of the "good people." If we, like Olivia, are looking for indicators of a person's moral character instead of an assessment of the situational factors at play, we are likely to respond differently to our email inboxes.

On the other hand, Olivia's experiences of feeling excluded on campus may have made her especially sensitive to the wording of the email. Most of us have our own experiences of reacting or overreacting

---

[6]Lukianoff and Haidt, *Coddling of the American Mind*, 54.
[7]Lukianoff and Haidt, *Coddling of the American Mind*, 85.

to an email, which allows us to empathize with Olivia's initial feelings. Instead of acting on those initial feelings, when we are trying to love people well (hopefully all the time) in assigning causes to their behavior (like labeling someone a racist), *we need to try to create conditions for good thinking* by removing distractions, asking for the opinions of other good thinkers, making sure we are not thinking under conditions of scarcity (get a snack if you need it), and then taking a moment to consider the big picture. Next, in cases like Olivia's, we should employ good thinking strategies like acknowledging an initial bias (she seems racist), embracing doubt (we could be wrong), practicing intellectual humility (we are not good at labeling people), assigning a probability (most people are not explicitly racist), and then considering the source of the facts that underlie my opinion (one email). I hope that I can have the humility to be slow to judge and quick to apologize. We all should do better to treat all people with love and respect. To do that, we all need to be willing to take the hit to self-esteem that happens when we all admit we all have the potential to behave in a way that appears racist, and we all have the potential to mislabel someone, so let's do our best to pursue accuracy and righteousness in our attributions.

ASSUME PEOPLE LIKE YOU WHEN YOU MAKE ATTRIBUTIONS

Beyond the pitfalls of failing to consider the power of a person's situation, and the lack of humility that comes from failing to consider the perceptions of others, *we are inaccurate because we also generally underestimate how much someone likes us.* I recently met a woman who I really wanted to get to know better and forge a friendship with. We were at a friend's pool and our children were playing. She had one child swimming, while I had three. While the interaction was happening, I was interrupted by phone calls from my husband and the awkward parenting moments that come from three children at a pool.

I didn't think too much about how I was being perceived while the interaction was happening, but in the middle of the night, I started to think about all the reasons she might have thought I was rude in that interaction. I managed to go back to sleep, but those feelings were still present in the morning. Then I remembered the research that makes me feel better when I have a vulnerability hangover.

Psychologist Erica Boothby writes about something she calls "the liking gap."[8] This refers to the bias that emerges after a conversation with a new person in which we underestimate how much the other person liked us. It seems counterintuitive based on some of the other biases included in this book that we would underestimate how much we are liked, but especially in conditions where we like someone we just met, we tend to think the other person might not have liked us as much as we liked them. In her first experiment, participants were paired with a member of the same gender, had a five-minute conversation in which they were given ice-breaker style questions like, "What are your hobbies?" and then independently answered questions regarding how much they liked the interaction partner and how much they thought the interaction partner liked them. Boothby found that participants liked their partners more than they thought their partners liked them, which is the definition of the liking gap. Interestingly, shy participants showed greater liking gaps than non-shy participants.

After establishing the effect, Boothby goes on to try to answer the question of why the liking gap exists. This experiment is similar to the first one but adds questions regarding what influenced the development of their perceptions. Questions like, "What are the top three moments from your conversation that caused you to form the impression of the other person that you did?" and "What are the top three moments that caused the other person to form the impression of you that he or she did?" They then rated the positivity and negativity

---

[8]Erica J. Boothby et al., "The Liking Gap in Conversations: Do People Like Us More Than We Think?," *Psychological Science* 29, no. 11 (2018): 1742-56.

of each of the three moments. It turned out that the negativity of those thoughts predicted a greater liking gap, which suggests that when we are busy judging our own behavior, we miss the positive cues that the other person is sending. She also tested whether the length of the conversation might matter. The lengths she measured included conversations from five minutes to forty-five minutes in length; the liking gap was identical in each condition. She also conducted a year-long longitudinal study with freshman suitemates, who rated their liking five times over the academic year. For these students the liking gap was present at every measurement except the final measurement. It is likely that given extended interaction over months of time, we become more accurate in assessing how much another person likes us.

So, given the "liking gap," it is probable that we all have experienced something Brené Brown calls a "vulnerability hangover."[9] This is the feeling we get when we think back over the interactions we have had with people and realize that we might have been perceived differently than we wanted to be perceived. These experiments remind us that most people are like me after the interaction with the woman at the pool, but in most cases, this is a bias and not reality. Instead of agonizing over how we are perceived, we are best served by sending clear signals to other people that we like them to reduce their liking gap, and to remember that we are likely biased in our own liking gap. At an even higher level, our identity is not tied to other people's perceptions so if we are able to remind ourselves of that, then maybe we can avoid the liking gap altogether.

When we talk about impression formation in class, I ask students to think about whether we should care at all about what other people think about us. Another person's perception of us has real consequences, and therefore, not to care about the impression is not to care about the

---

[9]Brené Brown, *The Power of Vulnerability: Teachings on Authenticity, Connection, and Courage* (Boulder, CO: Sounds True, 2012).

consequences. For example, if I choose not to care that I have hurt a friend's feelings because what I said was true, the consequences might be the loss of that relationship. My friend's impression of me has shifted from a trusted confidante who is sensitive to their concerns, to someone who will disregard their feelings. I may think that I have spoken the truth in love (Ephesians 4:15), but my perception is not shared by my friend. If their impression doesn't matter, then I should not concern myself with their response and take the loss of friendship as the natural consequence. If their impression does matter, then I should be moved to correct their impression through further explanation and a demonstration of love. In this type of context that most of us have experienced, it makes sense to assume that, of course, another person's impression should matter because we are supposed to love each other. On the other hand, someone who is fully motivated to cultivate a positive impression on others strikes us as lacking in integrity.

In 1 Corinthians Paul writes, "To the Jews, I became like a Jew, to win the Jews. . . . I have become all things to all people so that by all possible means I might save some" (1 Corinthians 9:20-22). This suggests that Paul understands how he is being perceived and he wants to break down the cultural barriers in others' perceptions of him in order to be persuasive to them for the sake of the gospel. I don't think that Paul is suggesting that his identity is found in pleasing people. His assessment of his own value is not tied to whether or not he fits in with the Jews, the Greeks, the weak, or the others mentioned in those verses. He is clear that this identity is for the sake of the gospel. It is because of his love for those people. He is motivated by love for others rather than love for self. If I am motivated to have others like me so that I can feel better about myself, it is my love for myself and not others that motivates me to care about the impression I make. If I think about the impression I am making on others for the purpose of loving them, to clearly and persuasively speak the truth in love to them, then my identity is not tied to their reception. The question is then not whether we should care about someone else's impression of us, but why a person's impression of us might matter. The answer ought to be that we care about other people's impressions because we care that other people feel loved.

If we want to pursue accuracy in our impressions of others and in the impressions we give of ourselves to others, we ought to be concerned with the data on accuracy. It turns out that under normal circumstances we aren't very accurate in our impressions of others. The term for this is the transparency bias,[10] which is the idea that we think other people can read our emotions better than they can. The transparency bias is the result of the larger self-bias where we think other people view the world with the same perspective that we do. Psychologists thought maybe this inaccuracy was an issue of motivation, so they paid people to increase their accuracy. That didn't work. Many of the things they tried didn't work. This is best exemplified in the data that show that married couples are most accurate in their ability to predict one another's thoughts when they are newlyweds; they get worse over time.[11] The argument is that married couples start to make assumptions, get lazier in their desire to predict the other person's thoughts and feelings, and rely on old information. "What do you mean, you don't like cabbage? You used to like cabbage, right?" "I did like cabbage about thirty years ago." Not surprisingly, the best way to increase accuracy is just to ask someone what they are thinking and feeling in specific situations. The perceiver needs to be more explicit in their approach, but the actor also should try to be more explicit by telling the perceiver what they are thinking and feeling. Turns out the best way to improve accuracy is to just be explicit all around. If you are afraid of being misperceived or misunderstood, explain how you are feeling and thinking explicitly. If you want

---

[10]Thomas Gilovich and Kenneth Savitsky, "The Spotlight Effect and the Illusion of Transparency," *Current Directions in Psychological Science* 8, no. 6 (1999): 165-68.

[11]Shankar Vedantam, "How to Know Another Person," September 19, 2022, in *Hidden Brain*, NPR, podcast, https://hiddenbrain.org/podcast/how-to-really-know-another-person.

to understand someone else, ask questions. Loving people means showing up and being as explicit as you can.

Returning to the interaction with the other mom at the pool—to think more accurately about our relationship, I need to *set up good conditions for thinking* and employ good strategies. Rather than thinking in the middle of the night, when I am experiencing a scarcity of sleep, it might be best to wait until I am well-rested. I might also consult another good thinker to get their opinion. I should also make sure I am not distracted and take a moment to consider the big picture of my life. Under these conditions, I should acknowledge my initial bias (to think that I like her more than she likes me). Then I should embrace doubt (given the liking gap data, it's possible she likes me more than I think she does). I should practice intellectual humility (I'm not that good at assigning causes to people's behavior). I should think probabilistically (most people don't have strong negative feelings toward me). I should also recognize the source of the facts that are informing my opinion (one interaction at a pool). After completing this process, I realized that I needed more information to conclude that she didn't like me, so it would be wisest for me to proceed assuming that she liked me and to give more explicit positive feedback in future interactions. *We can all improve the accuracy of our attributions by giving more explicit feedback.*

HELP YOUR NEIGHBOR LIKE YOU HELP YOURSELF

Beyond just being accurate in our attributions about other people, if we are trying to love our neighbors, we should help them. Luke chapter six says, "If you do good to those who are good to you, what credit is that to you? Even sinners do that. . . . But love your enemies, do good to them, and lend to them without expecting to get anything back" (Luke 6:32-35). I love this passage because it acknowledges human nature: that we are motivated to reciprocate. The reason we help others is often because we expect some type of payback later. If we are thinking about reciprocity, there won't be much altruism because reciprocity is not a selfless form of giving. *Pursuing accuracy ought to include not just reciprocity but altruism.* Starting the day by positioning the self relative to God and others ought to remind us that others are just like us and are deserving of our help. Studies that explore how and why people respond with heroism in life-threatening situations conclude that the people who do this are most likely relying on automatic thinking and have practiced the lifesaving behavior so that their bodies can rely on procedural memory in order to save another person in danger.[12] Fire-fighters and other first responders are not doing a complicated thought process to figure out what to do when there is a fire. I am humbled when I read the stories of these heroes because in most of the profiled situations, I have neither the knowledge nor the training to be able to rely on procedural memory to help. I am also grateful to the men and women who make that kind of training their life's work so that they are ready to do what needs to be done when heroic altruism is needed.

I don't think heroism is the only route to altruism. *Helping that results from slow thinking is possible and important and probably makes up the majority of helping behavior.* I hesitate to call helping altruism since the definition of altruism requires that the person helping is doing it with no ulterior motive other than to help. We are not good at judging the motives of people, so it becomes very difficult to assume a selfless motive to helping behavior of any kind. Re-searchers are more likely to assume altruism in life-threatening situations because the cost-benefit ratio that includes death tips the as-sessment to being selfless rather than selfish. I think the other reason we restrict the title of altruism for helping to heroic acts is that if a person has too long to consider whether or not to help (helping that results from slower thinking), it seems more likely that additional selfish motives will factor into the decision-making process.

---

[12]David G. Rand and Ziv G. Epstein, "Risking Your Life Without a Second Thought: Intuitive Decision-Making and Extreme Altruism," *PLoS ONE* 9, no. 10 (2014).

Given the high bar required for helping to qualify as altruism, it makes more sense to think about ways to encourage helping behavior, and to hope that the slow thinking that leads to the practice of helping can make helping behavior part of procedural memory and one day lead to fast thinking helping. Thus, the possibility of altruism is the result of a lot of slow thinking helping, like volunteering at a food bank or delivering a meal to a grieving family.

I was talking about altruism with a student when she described her current job situation. It was the beginning of September, and she was working at a golf course where most of the other summer workers had left for school. In her mind, she was thinking that she was really helping the golf course owner by staying on when most of the workers had left. As she was explaining to her boss that she was planning to start looking for other work, he gave a very supportive response, and it became clear to my student that her boss thought that he was helping her. I would guess that most of us have had the experience of thinking that we are the ones doing the helping only to recognize that we are receiving most of the benefit.

After describing the golf course situation, my student went on to talk about the drive-through phenomenon where one person starts to pay for the person behind them to start a chain of people doing the same thing. When you think about that phenomenon, it seems easy to identify the person who starts the helping process: it's the person at the front of the line who starts paying for an extra car. But isn't there some other helping that led to the economic privilege that put that person in a position where they were able to do that? All of us have been the receiver of benefits that make helping possible. I think my student is right that when we help, we often feel like we are the person at the front of the drive-through line. We wrongly believe that helping starts with us. We believe that our helping was a deliberate, generous, and possibly difficult choice.

Is there something wrong with thinking we are at the front of the drive-through line? Like most biases, there is a benefit to our self-esteem if we think we are the instigator of good things. This selfish motive, thinking that we are wonderful generous people, is a reward for helping and it motivates more helping. Anything that motivates more helping is not all bad. It just isn't entirely accurate to believe that we are the front of the drive-through line. Our helping is valuable, but we just can't be accurate in taking all the credit for it. We ought to help with gratitude toward the other people who helped us to even make the helping possible. It is accurate and incentivizing to me to think about honoring the people who have helped me by helping others. *In this way we can more accurately see ourselves as part of a shared humanity.* We are not better than the others we are helping, and the others who helped us are not better than we are. We are part of each other because of the reciprocity of helping across time and generations. We all benefit from the reciprocity of helping each other in ways we might not even fully know. Like the golf course owner and worker, it is not always clear who is the recipient and who is the helper. No one is at the front of the drive-through line, but we all ought to be helping regardless of the purity of our motives. Even if we are still practicing and never get to the automatic helping of altruism, we need to keep helping.

To *set up our environments to increase helping,* we should first get rid of distractions so that helping can be more of a habit.[13] It makes sense to schedule a regular time of volunteering so that it can become part of a regular daily or weekly behavior. We should surround ourselves with other people who regularly help. Volunteering with a group of friends makes it more fun and more like something everyone does. Thinking about how helping may make a difference far into the future will remind us of the big picture. Once we have set up conditions to make helping easier, *there are slow-thinking strategies that will make it more likely that we will choose to help.* It is worth acknowledging that there may be initial reactions that bias us against helping. I may tell

---

[13]Bibb Latané and John M. Darley, "Bystander 'Apathy,'" *American Scientist* 57, no. 2 (1969): 244-68.

myself that helping will be very uncomfortable and not very effective. It is worth taking the time to embrace doubt. It might be very uncomfortable, but I won't know until I actually help. I can be more intellectually humble and collect more information, acknowledging that I may not know whether helping will be uncomfortable or whether it will be effective until I learn more. I should try to think probabilistically. It is very unlikely that my helping will hurt someone. I should also consider the sources that inform my opinion about helping. I have had a few awkward helping situations in the past. After employing these strategies, it is most often the case that I ought to at least try to help. So hopefully, someday, helping could be my default, but for now, I may have to slow-think my way there.

NO ONE IS THAT MUCH MORE ATTRACTIVE THAN YOU ARE

Not only are we supposed to love our neighbors through knowing and helping them, but *if we are pursuing accuracy, we are supposed to love them when they aren't likeable.* Returning to Luke 6, before the helping sentence, it says "If you love those who love you, what credit is that to you? Even sinners love those who love them" (Luke 6:32). My attraction lecture is structured around a list of superficial characteristics that increase the probability of attraction (for example, physical attractiveness, similarity, proximity, and so on).[14] To get someone's attention, we have to communicate that we like them (reciprocal liking is a big predictor of attraction).[15] In order to get someone interested in us, we have to look good, show that we like them, be around them frequently, and communicate agreement. It sounds so simple and superficial. I frequently feel like I am an author of a nineties women's magazine trying to tell women how to get a man. I tell students, if this

---

[14]Shanhong Luo and Guangjian Zhang, "What Leads to Romantic Attraction: Similarity, Reciprocity, Security, or Beauty? Evidence from a Speed-Dating Study," *Journal of Personality* 77, no. 4 (2009): 933-64.

[15]Theodore M. Newcomb, "The Prediction of Interpersonal Attraction," *American Psychologist* 11, no. 11 (1956): 575-86.

all sounds superficial, it's because it is. It doesn't sound like the 1 Corinthians 13 version of love being patient, kind, and lacking envy (see
1 Corinthians 13:4). If the natural "love" file folder includes ways other
people can bless me with their presence through their humor or their
access to a beach house, how do I get a new "love" folder that can
include people who don't bless me with their presence and might even
make my life worse with their presence?

I had a friend who wanted to date someone who was blind because
she thought that the person would be less superficial. When I watched
a documentary on romantic love featuring blind singles,[16] I was so
excited because I was hoping to hear about how non-superficial
people who are blind are when it comes to judging what is attractive.
If you can't see someone's weight, you surely can't share our culture's
obsession with thinness. If you can't see someone's facial features, you
can't judge them based on the size of their eyes, the width of the smile,
the height of their cheekbones, or the symmetry of their features. You
can imagine my surprise when watching the documentary that I discovered that the blind singles were just as superficial as the rest of us.
They chose different features. They were more sensitive and judgmental regarding vocal features that were just as superficial. One
person featured in the documentary said, "I'm obsessed with what I
look like. My teeth have to feel a certain way. My face has to feel a
certain way. An outfit I put on has to feel a certain way. Being attractive makes it easier for people to look past my blindness." In retrospect, I should have realized this was the case when I consider how
quickly our brain adjusts to accommodate disability.[17]

The connection between the attractiveness data and stereotyping is
clear, even for people who are blind, when we realize that there is a
stereotype applied to physically attractive people called the halo effect

[16]*Blind Love*, directed by Patricia Zagarella (iTVS, 2020).
[17]Bryan Kolb and Robbin Gibb, "Brain Plasticity and Recovery from Early Cortical Injury," *Developmental Psychobiology* 49, no. 2 (2007): 107-18.

where attractiveness is linked to goodness.[18] I don't need to know your character because if you are attractive, I can just assume that you are good. This is similar to stereotypes for other groups that allow us to assume that if I know your group membership, I don't need to know your character, I can just assume you are evil, stupid, dangerous, and generally wrong about everything. Given these stereotypes, it makes sense that members of disadvantaged groups have tried to use attractiveness techniques to reduce the negative bias that is already present.

In graduate school, some friends of mine were interested in ways to reduce racial bias on the implicit association test.[19] For background, the implicit association test (IAT) is a reaction time-based test, developed by Mahzarin Banaji and a few others, to measure how quickly we associate good words and bad words with people representing different races. In my friends' experiment, a Black student either touched or didn't touch the participant before the participant took an IAT. The results revealed that there was a difference between those who were touched and those who were not touched. Participants who were touched showed less bias. The explanation is that touch is something that is shared with a person's ingroup; therefore, when the Black experimenter touches you, you feel more connected, and that connection extends to their group. I loved this experiment so much that it became the basis for a series of experiments I conducted on attitudes toward gay and lesbian couples. We found that men who were touched by other men in the course of an experiment were more comfortable with pictures of gay and lesbian couples, responded less negatively on an explicit measure of attitudes, and had a smaller bias favoring straight couples on an IAT.[20]

---

[18]Christopher G Wetzel, Timothy D Wilson, and James Kort, "The Halo Effect Revisited: Forewarned Is Not Forearmed," *Journal of Experimental Social Psychology* 17, no. 4 (1981): 427-39.

[19]Charles R. Seger, "Literal Intergroup Contact: Embodied Relational Cues and the Reduction of Intergroup Bias" (Doctoral diss., Indiana University, 2010).

[20]E. Devers, S. McEuen, A. Frueh, and A. Blankenship, "Reducing Sexual Prejudice Through Touch" (Paper, Midwestern Psychological Association annual meeting, Chicago, May 2012).

From these two experiments, it's clear that we can reduce bias when we do things to communicate affiliation, such as touching someone. When someone acts as though they like us, we like them, and if that person is a member of a disadvantaged group, that liking can get extended to other members of that group. "It is hard to hate up close" is a cliché for a reason. I recently listened to a podcast by a pastor describing his first experience with a gay member of his church. He described a situation in which he had accidentally outed the man to his family and entire congregation. The pastor recalls the humbling experience of apologizing and sitting with that man in his grief over the mistake. The man forgave the pastor.[21] Forgiveness is an ingroup behavior, so when it is extended across groups, it reduces bias.

One of the other things that strikes me both about these experiments and the list of ways to increase attractiveness is that members of disadvantaged groups feel even more pressure to increase their attractiveness. The pandemic has disrupted this somewhat, but in my academic circles, I am often struck by the White-male privilege of dressing down; women and minorities have to work harder to prove themselves and therefore need to use dress to communicate authority.[22] Likewise, White men have more latitude to express anger. Anger is viewed much more negatively when expressed by a woman or minority.[23] In part, I think this is because women and minorities have learned to use anger more infrequently, making it rare and noticeable when expressed. If women and minorities feel more pressure to communicate reciprocal liking and attractiveness, they are also feeling pressure to avoid telling the hard truth. We choose happy

[21]Brian McLaren, "Seeing Is a Social Act," in *Learning How to See*, October 12, 2020, Center for Action and Contemplation, podcast, https://cac.org/podcasts/2-seeing-is-a-social-act.

[22]Mara S. Aruguete, Joshua Slater, and Sekela R. Mwaikinda, "The Effects of Professors' Race and Clothing Style on Student Evaluations," *The Journal of Negro Education* 86, no. 4 (2017): 494-502.

[23]Jessica M. Salerno, Liana C. Peter-Hagene, and Alexander C. Jay, "Women and African Americans Are Less Influential When They Express Anger During Group Decision Making," *Group Processes & Intergroup Relations* 22, no. 1 (2017): 57-79.

stories told by attractive people,[24] rather than sad, true stories told by less-attractive people. So early on, we learn that to be heard we must be pretty and use sugar-coated words.

All of my daughters have asked why I wear makeup. It's hard for me to have a good reason for this behavior. I used to say, "It makes Mommy look less tired." This is true, but I think the real reason is because people will treat Mommy with more kindness and respect if she looks more like our cultural expectations of what women should look like. The other reason is that I have internalized this cultural expectation, so I feel better about myself when I more closely match it. These reasons, while true, don't feel great. Maybe I should try to force society to deal with me whatever my face looks like. On the other hand, a few minutes of makeup gives me better treatment and confidence, whether I like the reasons or not.

This story feels okay for makeup, but when the logic is extended to how we prefer to hear happy stories than true ones,[25] doing what is culturally preferred is not only wrong but dangerous. Just because our society prefers to hear happy stories told by people who are also simultaneously complimenting us doesn't mean that is the only information we should encounter. There are so many true and sad things. Not knowing the truth is not a sacrifice we should be making to feed our egos. We need to be better able to listen to the people who disagree with us[26] and who aren't always pleasant.

Let's return to the bigger question of how to love people who aren't constantly blessing us with their beauty and wit. We first need to *set up environments to be more loving.* We need to remove distractions and set up patterns of welcoming. For me, this may mean making

---

[24]Shelly Chaiken, "Communicator Physical Attractiveness and Persuasion," *Journal of Personality and Social Psychology* 37, no. 8 (1979): 1387-97.

[25]Kate C. McLean et al., "Redemptive Stories and Those Who Tell Them Are Preferred in the U.S.," *Collabra: Psychology* 6, no. 1 (2020).

[26]John C. Stapert and Gerald L. Clore, "Attraction and Disagreement-Produced Arousal," *Journal of Personality and Social Psychology* 13, no. 1 (1969): 64-69.

sure that I schedule a time to meet with each student, not just with students who are fun and interesting to me. We should surround ourselves with people who are good at loving a wide variety of people. We should set up reminders of the bigger picture of how welcoming a wide variety of people is more like the kingdom of God. *Once we have set up conditions, we should slow-think about the barriers to loving different people.* My bias, and probably yours, is to think that loving people who are not blessing me is hard. It is important to cast doubt on this statement. Sometimes it might be hard, but it might be worth it. Sometimes we might find out that there are ways that we are blessed by someone that wasn't obvious in the initial interaction. We need to stay intellectually humble and start getting to know people who may not look attractive in the first (or second or third) interaction. We can think probabilistically and recognize that most often, we are blessed when we get to know someone. We should also consider the sources that are informing our opinions. Usually, I am basing my opinion on one or two interactions. Now if this description of convincing yourself to love other people sounds selfish to you, you are probably right. It is also more likely to be accurate and may even eventually, after lots of practice, lead to a more automatic loving response toward people who aren't as obviously shiny and lovable as you are.

CHAPTER SIX SUMMARY

Attribution, altruism, and attraction are big and broad topics that are connected in the application of the ideas of this book thus far. If we are pursuing accuracy, we ought to consider how we are making attributions, helping, and loving others. Loving our neighbor is at the heart of each of these topics. In order to love our neighbor well in the attributions we make about them, we need to extend the Golden Rule beyond behavior to intentions. Assume the intentions of others to be the same as the intentions you would hold in their situation. Don't fall prey to the fundamental attribution error and make quick dispositional attributions for someone else's bad behavior. Love them enough to ask questions and fully understand their situation, recognizing that in the big scheme of things, no one has the moral high ground. Heroic altruism is often the result of automatic thinking, so we need to practice altruism with our controlled thinking so that we are ready for the moments of heroism. We also need to avoid scarcity mindsets in order to practice generosity. Believing that we have time and resources makes it more likely that we will help. Attraction occurs when we feel liked by someone, when we experience similarity with someone, when the relationship feels familiar, and when we receive benefits from the relationship. These are part of love—we are attracted to people who love us well. We should not get sidetracked by physical attraction but should look deeper to recognize the real love that is not connected to physical attraction. Love is different from niceness. Automatic thinking can confuse the two, so we need controlled thinking to recognize that love doesn't always come in affirmations; sometimes it comes with criticism. We need to remember our position relative to God and others, to see people as more like us, as deserving of our accurate knowledge of them, help, and love. In each of these cases, controlled thinking can help us live into our important values. Controlled thinking can help us love each other well. Hopefully, we can practice our way to automatic love, but until then, join me in my intentional helping that isn't quite altruism yet.

APPLICATION: UNBIASED NUDGES

- Be more generous in your attributions for others; consider how your actions might be perceived or misinterpreted. Err on the side of generosity in all your attributions, even if this requires controlled thinking.

- If you want to pursue accuracy in your attributions, ask people why they are doing things, and explain why you are doing things to others.

- Helping usually doesn't come automatically, so if you are waiting to feel like helping, you might never help. Use your controlled thinking to make helping a habit. Find a place to volunteer.

- We are automatically biased toward attractive things. Use controlled thinking to figure out what is true, even if it is not attractively packaged. Choose to get to know people who don't seem immediately attractive to you.

- We may not automatically behave in ways that are loving. Use controlled thinking to change your behavior, and your attitudes will likely fall in line.

SEVEN

REDUCING BIAS IN THE CHURCH

Within the "self" file folder, we also have subfolders for the group identities we hold, like "American" or "Christian" or "Star Wars fan." When we activate group identities, we behave differently than when only our individual identity subfolders are activated. The material we have covered so far may not help us in our collective behavior. *In order to pursue accuracy, we have to understand how group identities are different.* One of the things that distinguishes social psychology from other topics is the focus on how groups influence behavior. Mina Cikara, a group researcher, asks participants, 'When was the last time you punched someone?" to which most people respond, "Never." Similarly, she asks, "When was the last time you saw someone punch someone else in real life?" The answer to this is often never. As adults, we know we aren't supposed to punch other people or do things to harm people generally. This is part of a cultural norm that civilized societies implicitly adhere to. Mina Chikara goes on to point out that once a group identification, like your affiliation with your favorite sports team, gets activated, all bets are off—and someone might throw a punch.[1] The data support this anecdote. Consider the following as an example of the effect of group identification: participants who made a group decision regarding how much hot sauce to administer punished people with more hot sauce than people

---

[1]Shankar Vedantam, "Separating Yourself from the Pack," July 11, 2022, in *Hidden Brain*, NPR, podcast, https://hiddenbrain.org/podcast/separating-yourself-from-the-pack.

who made the decision alone.[2] Groups give people a cover to behave in ways that they ordinarily wouldn't.

WE ARE LESS BIASED WHEN WE REMEMBER WE ARE IN THE SAME GROUP

Just putting people in groups changes what we think. From a young age, kids learn that the purpose of groups is to create teams for competition. There is a line of social psychological research that is termed the "minimal groups paradigm."[3] In these experiments, participants are divided into groups based on a superficial designator like a preference for the color red over the color blue. In the classic version, participants were asked to estimate how many dots were on a screen, and then the experimenter would categorize the participants as being a "dot overestimator" or a "dot underestimator." These superficial divisions are enough to make participants start to favor members of the ingroup (like a fellow "dot overestimator") and to discriminate against members of the outgroup (like a "dot underestimator"). The "minimal groups paradigm" has been used in many experiments.[4] Tayla Lazerus and colleagues randomly assigned participants to wear either green shirts or blue shirts and then asked them to rate the valence of the expressions of members of their ingroup (based on shared shirt color) and members of the outgroup (wearing the non-shared shirt color). What they found is evidence for a positivity bias. That, regardless of the emotional expression of the face, participants rated the ingroup members' faces as more positive. We assign even superficially based ingroup members more points, more positive evaluations, more empathy, and as demonstrated in the experiment described above, more

[2]Brian P. Meier and Verlin B. Hinsz, "A Comparison of Human Aggression Committed by Groups and Individuals: An Interindividual-Intergroup Discontinuity," *Journal of Experimental Social Psychology* 40, no. 4 (2004): 551-59.

[3]Michael Billig and Henri Tajfel, "Social Categorization and Similarity in Intergroup Behaviour," *European Journal of Social Psychology* 3, no. 1 (1973): 27-52.

[4]Billig and Tajfel, "Social Categorization and Similarity in Intergroup Behaviour."

emotional positivity. All the positive attributions given to the ingroup are not bad by themselves, but the relative preference disadvantages the outgroup.[5]

The idea that people experience emotions differently when they are part of a group was a question that excited me when I was in graduate school. The professor of my class on stereotyping and prejudice had authored "intergroup emotions theory."[6] This work postulated that group emotions not only prompted violent behavior, such as punching people at sporting events, but could also prompt more extreme violent behavior like genocide. At the time that I was taking this class, I was leading a small group at my duplex. An Albanian PhD student, who was studying physics, approached me at church and asked me to lead a small group with him. He chose me because I was female and American, and thus would allow us to attract other graduate students who were both international and American. Our group identifications were salient right from the start. This group became very close. Abaz (my Albanian co-leader) met his wife in our group, and we prayed together for him to discover a particle, which he did. His story is just one of the stories of people who benefited from the close bonds that developed in our group.

I began thinking that group emotions must be benefiting us, not just increasing our tendencies to behave violently. I designed a very simple, clean experiment to test this idea. Participants were pretested for their emotions, self-esteem, and life satisfaction, and then, depending on their randomly assigned condition, were asked to write about a time when they felt happy, sad, angry, or anxious. Half of the participants in each of those four conditions had the addition of "as a member of a group." Then all the participants re-rated their emotions,

---

[5]Talya Lazerus et al., "Positivity Bias in Judging Ingroup Members' Emotional Expressions," *Emotion* 16, no. 8 (2016): 1117-25.
[6]Eliot R. Smith, Charles R. Seger, and Diane M. Mackie, "Can Emotions Be Truly Group Level? Evidence Regarding Four Conceptual Criteria," *Journal of Personality and Social Psychology* 93, no. 3 (2007): 431-46.

self-esteem, and life satisfaction. What I found was that participants in the happy conditions did not differ between the group and individual conditions. They all felt a lot better after reflecting on a happy experience. Participants in the anxiety conditions did not differ between the group and individual conditions either. While those in both of the sadness conditions felt lower levels of life satisfaction after describing the experience, those in the group condition did not experience the same level of decline as those in the individual condition did. Group identification made sad experiences less sad. Anger, as my professor would have predicted, was the most interesting. Experiencing anger alone led to a decrease in life satisfaction, but describing a shared anger-provoking experience led to an increase in life satisfaction that did not differ from the increase experienced by those in the happiness conditions. Just to test the strength of this result, I conducted a second experiment in which I again pretested for emotions, life satisfaction, and self-esteem but then had participants read an angry or sad story in which I had manipulated the pronouns to be either singular or plural. When the pronouns are plural in the angry story, participants showed the same increase in life satisfaction.

These preliminary experiments led to my dissertation work. I conducted a series of experiments where I created groups in the lab and manipulated their emotions. What I found mirrored the results of the first experiments. Anger experienced together feels good. In groups, anger tends to motivate behavior and having the group gives participants a greater perception of resources to combat the source of the anger. I should state here that these experiments were done exclusively with women because the data on social support is unequivocal in demonstrating the benefits of social support for women, but not for men.[7] Anecdotally, it is the explanation I give when my husband points out that women have gotten really good at raising money and

---

[7]Shelley E. Taylor, "Social Support: A Review," in *The Oxford Handbook of Health Psychology*, ed. Howard S. Friedman (Oxford: Oxford University Press, 2011), 190-214.

awareness for breast cancer research, but men have been less organized in fundraising for male specific cancers.

We value our groups. We treat group members with more kindness
and generosity.[8] They help us feel more powerful when we are angry
and less sad when we are devastated. In contrast, we treat people who
aren't in our groups with less kindness and generosity, sometimes
with venom and animosity. *To think in a less-biased way collectively,*
we need to expand our group to include everyone. We need to start the
day positioning the self to God and to others. The others who are
similar to us are not just the members of our Star Wars fan club, they
are all people on the planet. We need to activate a "children of God"
file folder that recognizes that all of us belong. Likewise, when
someone behaves badly, we need to activate the "sinners saved by
grace" file folder to which we all belong. If we want to pursue accuracy,
we need to practice activating the true identity that we share with
everyone else on the planet.

WE ARE LESS BIASED WHEN WE THINK COLLECTIVISTICALLY

In addition to being in groups, we exist within cultures. *In order to*
pursue accuracy, we have to understand the bias of our own culture.
One of the major cultural differences Americans recognize when they
leave the United States is the extreme individualism that characterizes
our society. One of the major benefits of travel, even if it's just through
books, is that it leads us to examine the cultural water that we are
swimming in. I have spent a considerable amount of time thinking
about what constitutes American culture and specifically evangelical
American culture.

It was surprising and helpful for me to realize while reading *Reading*
the Times by Jeffrey Bilbro that I have a culturally based assumption

---

[8]Henri Tajfel and John C. Turner, "The Social Identity Theory of Intergroup Behavior," in *Political*
Psychology: Key Readings, ed. John T. Jost and Jim Sidanius (New York: Psychology Press, 2004).

that progress bends toward justice.[9] This assumption is something I absorbed not just from American culture, but also American Christian culture. What this means is that when I read the news and learn about something that jeopardizes democracy or justice, I am not only sad, I am outraged. I am outraged in the way that suggests that implicitly I believe that we as a culture deserve to have things get better, and it is an egregious violation of my rights to have things get worse. Without this assumption that things are supposed to be getting better and more just, my emotional response would be less extreme. The author argues that this outrage is fueling political polarization. If I believe that my political party holds the keys to progress, but is being impeded by the opposing party, the level of outrage I feel over a political loss is likely to be much stronger than if I believe progress is not likely to happen regardless of who is in power. We even experience pleasure when the opposing political party loses politically even if it means all of us experience the negative economic effects of a decision like raising taxes or entering a war.[10] The pain in my pocketbook is not nearly as powerful as the joy of watching my political opponents lose. Winning and losing holds power over emotional responses if progress is the assumed trajectory of history and if my political party is believed to be the vehicle of progress.

Just as deeply held beliefs are influenced by culture, personality-trait words have also been applied to cultures. While most personality tests may not be well supported by evidence, there is a great deal of evidence on what we might describe as the personality of the United States. Gert Jan Hofstede inherited a longitudinal study from his father (this would be a great thing but unusual thing to inherit, right?). The study began in 1967 with his father collecting survey and interview data from all

---

[9]Jeffrey Bilbro, *Reading the Times: A Literary and Theological Inquiry into the News* (Downers Grove, IL: InterVarsity Press, 2021), 69.

[10]David J. Y. Combs et al., "Politics, Schadenfreude, and Ingroup Identification: The Sometimes Happy Thing About a Poor Economy and Death," *Journal of Experimental Social Psychology* 45, no. 4 (2009): 635-46.

the employees of IBM from all over the world and then conducting a factor analysis on the data. Factor analysis is a way to find patterns in the questions based on the numbers without applying any theory to it. Then when you find a "factor," which is just a group of questions that go together, you look at the questions and think about what might be the connecting idea between them. What he found was that there were clearer patterns between countries than there were based on job descriptions, gender, or seniority in the company. The data resulted in four factors or dimensions: individualism and collectivism, power distance, masculinity and femininity, and uncertainty avoidance. Since then, two more dimensions were added: long-term and short-term thinking, and indulgence and restraint.[11]

Just like the experience of taking a personality test, most of us have a pretty good idea of how our country might score on these dimensions, but we might not realize what the implications of the dimensions might be. On the first one, there is little doubt that most of us have enough insight into our culture to recognize our individualism. Based on the IBM data, the United States is the most individualistic culture on the planet. The implications of this are profound as it relates to the self. Most of the social psychological research is on WEIRD people, which stands for Western, Educated, Industrialized, Rich and Developed/Democratic. When I teach, or as I write this book, I know that I am presenting data that really only applies to a small number of people relative to the world's population, but also that most of the people who are in my classroom fall into the WEIRD category themselves. WEIRD is the water we are swimming in together. For one lecture, after presenting all the data on the self biases, I present data to answer the question of how far the biases generalize outside of the WEIRD population. If I were to summarize the data and the lecture, the bottom line is that the more individualistic the country, the more

---

[11]Gert Jan Hofstede, "Culture's Causes: The Next Challenge," *Cross Cultural Management* 22, no. 4 (2015): 545-69.

likely its citizens are to hold a strong independent view of the self, which will make the self more vulnerable, which will lead to a stronger need to employ self-esteem enhancing techniques.

Consider whether you think your success in life depends on your own abilities or help from others. If you strongly believe that your success depends on your abilities, then in order to believe that you will be successful, you need to believe that you have high abilities. This makes failure not just something that happens from time to time, but a reflection of who you are and your ability to succeed in the future. Recall the discussion in chapter three of a cute finding called the above-average effect. When Americans are asked to rate their sense of humor, attractiveness, ability to get along well with others, intelligence, and so on, compared to the average person, the results demonstrate that most people think of themselves as above average even though this is statistically impossible. This effect makes so much sense to me because we are probably not getting enough data on other people to be really accurate in making this assessment, so given that absence of good data, we err on the side of assumed superiority, which makes us feel good about ourselves. We aren't deliberately misrepresenting our intelligence, we are just interpreting what data we do have in our favor. I am honestly surprised that participants from collectivistic cultures, who have a more interdependent view of the self, don't show this effect. First-generation Canadian immigrants from East Asia did not show this effect, but their children did. The effect for these second-generation Canadians was not as strong as it was for the Canadians who did not have an immigrant parent, which suggests that the more time spent in an individualistic culture, the greater the need to self-enhance.[12]

In a real sense, those who grow up in a collectivist culture and develop a more interdependent view of the self, have established an

---

[12]Elanor F. Williams and Thomas Gilovich, "Do People Really Believe They Are Above Average?," *Journal of Experimental Social Psychology* 44, no. 4 (2008): 1121-28.

identity at which it is harder (though not impossible) to fail. Thus, like thinking about one's identity as a child of God, thinking of one's identity primarily as a member of a group from which you cannot be expelled reduces the biases designed to maintain self-esteem. Failure at work could more easily be explained situationally for someone from a collectivist culture than it could for someone from an individualistic culture. Americans are more likely to look for reasons that the person deserved to be fired; whereas someone from India might be more likely to think about situational forces. In this regard, those who come from collectivist cultures should be better situated to do what I am suggesting in this book, which is to pursue accuracy with less bias because self-esteem maintenance pressures have been reduced. In one regard, I think this is true, which is what feels very appealing about a collectivist culture. On the other hand, there is more pressure to fit in. Belonging to a collectivist culture means that the worst failure that is to be feared is rejection by one's family or community.

In an experiment comparing Americans to Japanese participants, Japanese participants who were randomly assigned to write about a failure situation were more likely to consider the failure situation to be self-relevant than the Americans who wrote about failure. When all participants judged the positivity and negativity of the stories, the failure stories written by Japanese participants were judged to have a bigger negative impact on self-esteem than the failure stories written by Americans.[13] This suggests that the Japanese participants, and likely other members of more collectivist cultures, are more open to self-criticism with the goal of fitting into the group. In this regard, failure is still threatening, but only insofar as group membership is jeopardized.

This data makes the argument that perhaps we would be more accurate thinkers in a collectivistic culture because we would have less

---

[13]Toshitake Takata, "Self-Enhancement and Self-Criticism in Japanese Culture," *Journal of Cross-Cultural Psychology* 34, no. 5 (2003): 542-51.

of a need to artificially boost self-esteem. In order to create a more collectivistic culture, we need to deepen our relationships and increase our sense of social belonging. Vivek Murthy, US Surgeon General, has been writing and speaking on the topic of loneliness as an epidemic.[14] We need to belong,[15] and that lack of belonging can be thought of in different dimensions. We can feel lonely because of a lack of deep personal connections with close confidantes, we can feel lonely because of a deficit of friends to do things with, and we can feel collective loneliness because we don't have a community to belong to. In *Bowling Alone*, the author argues that it is this last type, the collective loneliness, that is growing. Interestingly, *Bowling Alone* was written before social media, and since many of our forms of social connection went online, one might argue that the belonging that comes from groups has gotten even rarer since the early 2000s, when that book was published.[16] Given the deficit of in-real-life groups, it is not surprising that people have tied a great deal of identity to their online groups or political affiliations, which can exist in the absence of real interaction and depth of relationship with others.

The church can still offer a remedy for collective loneliness. The work of former Harvard Divinity School fellow Casper ter Kuile explores how ritual is connected to feelings of belonging.[17] Church and religion generally is one place where rituals and belonging can flourish. He argues that some of the explanation for the power of ritual is in the reading of sacred texts. As an atheist, he doesn't use the Bible as sacred text, but instead created large groups of Harry Potter

[14]Vivek H. Murthy, *The Healing Power of Human Connection in a Sometimes Lonely World* (New York: HarperCollins, 2020).

[15]Roy F. Baumeister and Mark R. Leary, "The Need to Belong: Desire for Interpersonal Attachments as a Fundamental Human Motivation," in *Interpersonal Development*, ed. Brett Laursen and Rita Zukauskiene (New York: Routledge, 2017), 57-89.

[16]Robert D. Putnam, *Bowling Alone: The Collapse and Revival of American Community* (New York: Simon and Schuster, 2000).

[17]Casper ter Kuile and Angie Thurston, *Where We Belong: Mapping American Religious Innovation* (Kalamazoo, MI: Fetzer Institute, 2015).

reading groups, which started functioning like the church for people during the pandemic.[18] In Denmark, one of the happiest countries on the planet, adults belong to an average of 2.5 social groups or clubs. In considering the work of Casper ter Kuile and others, I am reminded that the church must meet real social support needs of people, a role that first captured my psychological imagination when writing my dissertation.

In addition to increasing our social connectedness, another way to think more collectivistically is to think less often in terms of maximizing financial outcomes and more in terms maximizing social outcomes. When we are thinking about money, we focus on our independence and less on our interdependence. Thinking about money reduces altruism.[19] Thinking about money in order to be responsible with resources is important, but thinking about it too much may limit generosity. When the leaders of our academic and religious institutions are primed to think about money, assuming they behave like most of the rest of us, then they are less likely to think about the communal implications of their decisions and may be less generous in their approach. The danger of money primes is one that deserves more attention because it can work against other important values like caring for one another. It's hard to avoid thinking about financial outcomes if it is an important value in our culture, but in order to be righteous, we have to try to limit those thoughts to what is necessary to be good stewards of our resources.

A third way to think more collectivistically is to reduce our focus on differences between people. In order to imperfectly model what I am suggesting, I am going to write something that might offend everyone reading this book. I think it is okay to not have a strong

---

[18]Abigail Packard, "Harry Potter and the Sacred Text," *Children's Book and Media Review* 37, no. 12 (2016): 20.

[19]Eugene M. Caruso, Nicole L. Mead, and Kathleen D. Vohs, "There's No 'You' in Money: Thinking of Money Increases Egocentrism," *ACR North American Advances* 36 (2009): 206-9.

opinion on every hot button topic. Most of us are not experts on all hot button topics but feel like we need to have an opinion regardless of how well-informed or ill-formed the opinion is. So given that we don't have time to create a well-informed opinion, we just borrow the opinion of our social group. I am part of the group, the group is good, since they hold this position, I will adopt their opinion. Instead, it would be better to just admit that we haven't thought about something enough to render a definitive opinion, but that we are open to listening to others' opinions regardless of their group memberships. Everything doesn't have to be a dividing factor that could cause someone to lose their job. Some topics can include open questions about which there is room to hold different well-informed opinions. There ought to be room for those of us without well-informed opinions to admit that we don't know enough yet.

Thinking collectivistically does not necessarily eliminate bias, especially if we are trying to think more collectively while living in an individualistic culture. The same types of biases that affect us individually also affect us collectively; there is a social confirmation bias,[20] which mirrors the individual form of confirmation bias underpinning the echo chamber of ideas we encounter on social media. Extending the fundamental attribution error beyond making a dispositional attribution about the person to make a dispositional attribution for that person's whole social group is called the ultimate attribution error.[21] The fast thinking that affects us individually to make complex ideas into simple ones is the same fast thinking that can occur when thinking collectivistically.

In the same way that we need to individually consider the complexity of ideas and leave room to not know and room to disagree, we

---

[20]Joshua Klayman, "Varieties of Confirmation Bias," *Psychology of Learning and Motivation* 32 (1995): 385-418.

[21]Miles Hewstone, "The 'Ultimate Attribution Error'? A Review of the Literature on Intergroup Causal Attribution," *European Journal of Social Psychology* 20, no. 4 (1990): 311-35.

need to figure out how to do this collectively. We don't learn to engage with ideas if we cancel them. Universities can't encourage critical thinking if professors only present ideas that everyone already agrees are innocuous. The kind of humility that is required to use thinking strategies described in chapter five is hard to find as a collective value in today's academy or church, and definitely not found in today's politics. Humility seems like the only way forward for us individually and collectively. *Given that the values of culture bias thinking, we need to acknowledge that our individualistic culture will pressure us to prove our worth in ways that might cause us to use a self-bias to prop up our self-esteem. We need to meditate over and over on our position relative to God and others, so that we can affirm our value and the value of the people around us. Only then can we favor accuracy and righteousness over self-esteem in a culture that values individual accomplishment over a shared identity as children of God.*

WE MUST REDUCE IMPLICIT RACIAL BIAS

As much as I want to encourage us to open file folders that include all humans as part of our group, it is hard to avoid thinking about the ways people are different from us. Threats to belonging are everywhere. Any indicator that is used to separate people into "us" and "them" is a potential threat. The more important the "us" is to a person's identity, the more likely a person is to use that group identity to sort and judge other people.[22] *In order to pursue accuracy, we have to consider the implicit bias of our group identity.* Consider the implications of having a "self" file folder. Things that are important to a sense of self and identity are the file folders that are chronically activated. The implication of the chronic activation of a file folder is that it will be used to judge others. If I am chronically activating my identity as a professor, I am likely to quickly sort and judge other women as similar to myself

---

[22]Mina Cikara and Jay J. Van Bavel, "The Neuroscience of Intergroup Relations," *Perspectives on Psychological Science* 9, no. 3 (2014): 245-74.

based on their professions. If I hold a very strong identity as a vegan, it is likely that I will ask questions regarding other people's dietary decisions early on in a friendship so that I can judge similarity. Similarity is a major force in attraction,[23] so it makes sense that we use our important identities to sort out potential friends and confidantes. Our group identities are signals of similarity, and we will use our fast thinking to sort people quickly as part of our ingroups or outgroups.

When I think about how Jesus loved the other, the least of these, I am completely intimidated. Our human inclination to sort people based on similarity is strong and happens below awareness. Explicitly, I can explain why we should love everyone. I can explain, or try to at least, as I do throughout this book, that we should try to reduce the use of meaningless file folders to define ourselves and others. I argue that our identity should not be primarily based in the categories at which we can fail but should instead be found in our status as children of God and sinners saved by grace. Reducing implicit bias takes years and years of practice. I am recommending something that I have not been able to fully realize in my own life. If I had to put a number on it, as I recommend you do, I would only give myself a 5 percent on my ability to use my explicit knowledge of how things should be to change my implicit biases. I know what I should do, as Paul writes, but "I do what I do not want to do" (Romans 7:20). When I write about implicit bias in the context of groups, I do so as one who can try to explicitly explain how it should be *and* recognizes that how it should be is not even close to how I live my everyday life.

Implicit bias exists for all group membership markers, and its effects have been particularly damaging in the context of race. As a White person in a majority White context on the topic of implicit racial bias, I have been privy to conversations in which other White people dismiss racism as a thing of the past that does not apply to

---

[23]Christopher G. Wetzel and Chester A. Insko, "The Similarity-Attraction Relationship: Is There an Ideal One?," *Journal of Experimental Social Psychology* 18, no. 3 (1982): 253-76.

them. Explicit racial bias is much easier to spot, and this is what most White people are talking about when they make dismissive statements about racism. This is not what I am describing here. Implicit racial bias is not hatred, and it is much harder to spot. It is often measured in reaction time, such as in the favoritism toward White faces on the implicit association test (IAT). A bias does not mean that you even dislike other races; you just have more built-up positive associations with your own race. There is a bias toward similarity.

Rather than focusing on anecdotes, I'm going to describe three sets of experiments that drive home the point that implicit bias is antithetical to the Christian message on how to love each other and that implicit racial bias is nearly impossible to avoid. Implicit racial bias is impossible to avoid because we start learning it as preschoolers by watching the people around us model it nonverbally. Preschoolers who watched a video in which one character received more positive nonverbal signals were more likely to favor the individual favored in the video and then generalize that favoritism to others who were racially similar to the one favored in the video.[24]

In case you think that most preschoolers are not exposed to people who nonverbally prefer particular races, consider that most people who watch TV are also exposed to the nonverbal preferencing of White characters. Participants were exposed to scenes from eleven popular TV shows in which one character in a dialogue was edited out of the scene, and then participants were asked to judge how positively or negatively the missing character (edited-out character) was treated by the unedited character. Participants rated the nonverbal treatment of the unedited character to be more positive toward the edited-out White characters than the edited-out Black characters. After establishing that the shows model nonverbal bias favoring

---

[24]Allison L. Skinner, Andrew N. Meltzoff, and Kristina R. Olson, "'Catching' Social Bias: Exposure to Biased Nonverbal Signals Creates Social Biases in Preschool Children," *Psychological Science* 28, no. 2 (2016): 216-24.

White over Black characters, the authors had participants take a race IAT. As described in chapter six, an IAT is a computer-based test that compares the reaction time it takes to pair good words with White faces, good words with Black faces, bad words with White faces, and bad words with Black faces. Participants that had more exposure to the TV shows had higher IAT scores. It turns out that just watching TV shows in 2008 was enough to increase implicit bias.[25]

Nonverbal bias is something that we could choose to dismiss as small, but I would urge you to consider that in the case of the implicit bias toward Black faces, the bias is not just to show less preference to Black faces, but to dehumanize them. A series of experiments has demonstrated the link between Black faces and apes. In the first experiment, participants (sixty White; sixty-one non-White) are subliminally primed with fifty Black male faces, fifty White male faces, or fifty line-drawings. After the priming, participants were presented with fuzzy pictures of animals that increase in clarity over time. They were told to press a button on the computer keyboard as soon as they could identify the animal. Participants who received the Black face prime were faster at identifying the apes, but not the non-ape animals. Subsequent studies further established that this implicit connection exists and that the participants did not explicitly connect "apes" with the Black stereotype. Most disturbingly, participants who were primed with ape-words (*monkey, chimp, baboon, orangutan*, and so on) as opposed to big-cat words (*lion, tiger, panther, puma*, and so on) were more likely to approve of police violence against a Black suspect. The implicit connection between Blacks and apes is not just evidence for implicit bias, *but for the dehumanization of an entire group of people.* The title of this article, "Not Yet Human" speaks to the wrongness of this association.[26]

---

[25]Max Weisbuch, Kristin Pauker, and Nalini Ambady, "The Subtle Transmission of Race Bias via Televised Nonverbal Behavior," *Science* 326, no. 5960 (2009): 1711-14.

[26]Phillip Atiba Goff et al., "Not Yet Human: Implicit Knowledge, Historical Dehumanization, and

I describe these experiments here because I think we have to sit with the idea that group-based implicit bias is real, it is nearly impossible to avoid, and it has dehumanizing consequences. It would be wrong for me to suggest that this is something that could be overcome easily. This is where we start. It is important to acknowledge and grapple with the intransigent nature of implicit racial bias. It's important to think about the cost of difference, of racism, of sexism, of dehumanization wherever it exists. I recommend doing more reading on this topic because of the weightiness. The feeling of weight ought to come through listening to the stories of the people around us, through reading the news, through reading the Bible, and being alive to the difficult realities that people are facing.

BEING A LESS-BIASED CHURCH

While I am a social psychologist, I am not a theologian. I know enough to know that we are not fully practicing the teachings of Jesus on this topic. The radical love of Jesus for the other is something we know explicitly. I teach it explicitly. I talk about it explicitly (the only way to talk about it or teach it). I make explicit moves to love people who are different from me, but I am not unconditionally loving or unbiased in my love for others.

Jesus calls us to love the least of these. A few years ago, my daughters got lice—presumably from school. A Sunday school teacher alerted me that my four-year-old was scratching her head and thought I should check her for lice. My husband scoured the internet trying to figure out what we should do. We tried the at-home remedies but then found out that there are places you can go to (one-hour plus drive for us) to delouse your child for a fee. In exchange we would get a guarantee that the lice would be gone (or they will offer a second free treatment). While we were there paying more than one hundred

---

dollars per head, I started asking questions about the process, and realized that I could start a lice treatment center in my town that would be free. This began a years-long process of conducting a needs assessment, procuring a location (thank you, BORN Church), getting a grant, recruiting volunteers, and launching the "Grant County Lice Treatment Project." For two years now, I have been treating lice and collecting data on stigma with the help of student volunteers. When I recruit students, I tell them that this is a high-benefit volunteering opportunity because they will get the satisfaction of helping someone with something really needed.

Within the first few weeks we were open, a little person came to our lice treatment center. Sam, the engineering genius who did all the renovation work for the center and helped create the lice treatment devices, realized that he was too short to get into our salon chairs and too heavy for our college students to lift. Within the ten minutes it takes for us to explain the treatment and have him sign the waiver, Sam had used his tools and leftover lumber to make a stepstool for him to get in the chair so that we wouldn't have to make the situation any more awkward for him. He had one of the worst cases of lice we have ever seen.

A few days later, I was retelling this story to my psychology professor colleagues at a department meeting. One of them turned to me and with an emotional voice said that what we were doing for people at the lice clinic was just like Jesus touching the lepers. Let me just say, no, this is not like Jesus touching the lepers. As much as I am endlessly impressed by Sam and his ability to see what needs to be done and engineer a solution for it, the only way this is like Jesus touching the lepers is that people who are on the receiving end of stigma got treatment. In both cases people were helped. That is where the similarity ends. The motivations and attitudes of Jesus are very different from mine. I treat lice for selfish reasons. I get great satisfaction out of helping. I like that I am helping people with something that is not hard to fix but can have great benefits. I also like to explicitly endorse the idea of interacting with people who are different from me. Lice do not discriminate based on socioeconomic status—lice just like warm heads—but the people who come to receive treatment are often on the lower end of the socioeconomic spectrum. When we interact, all my stereotypes get activated. I assess socioeconomic status within the first moments of the interaction. That socioeconomic file folder biases the entire interaction. Jesus' file folder for the poor is different from mine.

In most areas of my life, I have self-selected to remain in environments where people are a lot like me. These people are easier to love because similarity naturally attracts.[27] Jesus tells us that even sinners love those that love them, but that we are called to love our enemies and do good to those who hate us (Luke 6:27). I have a hard time just loving the people who are different from me. I have to use controlled explicit thinking to do what is right—to give money to charities, to volunteer my time, or to show up for people I don't particularly like. I want to be more like Jesus. I want my implicit bias to push me to love all people. I want that for all of us.

As I think about the collective self, and how important it is to belong, I think about a conversation I had with my daughter. My eight-year-old had a pensive look on her face, so I asked what she was thinking about, and she said, "I feel different from other kids. I don't fit in." As she said it, there were two conflicting messages that traveled across my mind, "Who cares what the other kids think? You are amazing! You don't need to fit in" and, "You will have friends, let me help you figure out how to fit in." Neither conversation is particularly useful because those messages make the story about the kids and not her. I thought for longer than it took for those first two ideas to appear in my mind, looked into her eyes and said, "In all the ways that really

---

[27]Wetzel and Insko, "The Similarity-Attraction Relationship."

matter, you are just like the other kids. You are a child of God and a sinner saved by grace just like they are, so when you get down to the things that really matter, you can connect. In many other superficial ways, you are different from other kids. Celebrate those differences. Be the best version of you that you can be. Don't stop being yourself but recognize that you can connect with others because you have deep human things in common."

All of us, like my eight-year-old, want to fit in, to be accepted, to be liked, but as adults we all realize that fitting in for its own sake is not the goal; the goal is belonging.[28] So when we change our values or bodies to fit in, we feel more alone. We belong when we connect across the deep sameness we share and celebrate the less deep differences between us that make life interesting. The message that we are all alike more than we think, we connect through our sameness, and we hold differences a little less tightly is the message of this chapter and one of the best strategies I know to reduce bias. If we are more alike than different, it follows that we ought to be able to act in the best interest of the group, a group that includes all of us. Acting in the best interest of the group might benefit the individual because of the interconnectedness of our world. *It then follows that thinking about the self as part of a bigger whole is a more accurate way to view the self.*

CHAPTER SEVEN SUMMARY

To pursue accuracy, we must understand how group identities are different. Given that group identities can benefit those within them, we need to expand our group to include everyone, because we are all part of the most important group identity: being children of God and sinners saved by grace. We also need to recognize the bias introduced by our culture: specifically, the individualistic nature of our culture as

---

[28]Matthew J. Hornsey and Jolanda Jetten, "The Individual Within the Group: Balancing the Need to Belong with the Need to Be Different," *Personality and Social Psychology Review* 8, no. 3 (2004): 248-64.

Americans. Individualism increases our need to prop up self-esteem to prove our individual worth, which will work against our pursuit of accuracy. By thinking about ourselves as part of a larger collective, we can reduce some of the pressure to succeed individually and be better able to focus on a shared identity. Group identities result in a bias to affiliate with similar others. Implicit racial bias can lead to dehumanization. We need to promote belonging, not by ignoring difference, but by connecting in our sameness and celebrating our differences.

APPLICATION: UNBIASED NUDGES

- Think of a way to regularly remind yourself that all humanity belongs in your group.

- Acknowledge the biasing forces of your culture. Try to behave in a countercultural way by giving people in our groups the freedom to be wrong, to be ambivalent, and to be uncertain about their views.

- Celebrate the deep similarity that is shared across humanity.

CONCLUSION

SELF-COMPASSION

IN THE BEGINNING OF THIS BOOK, I made the argument that we want to feel good about ourselves, and therefore, we are willing to trade accuracy and even righteousness for self-esteem. In some situations, we are compelled to choose accuracy over self-esteem because we are very motivated to avoid a repeat of negative outcomes. I suggest that having an identity that is focused on things at which we cannot fail removes the constant threat to self-esteem that works against accuracy. Specifically, from a Christian perspective, I argue that being beloved children of God and sinners saved by grace ought to be central to identity. That identity is not threatened by any form of failure. It is important to remind ourselves that we are beloved children of God when failure is looming so that we can, if not embrace failure, at the very least acknowledge it and learn from it. We need to regularly open the identity subfolder marked "child of God."

On the other hand, when our tendency is to dwell on failure and ruminate on regrets, thinking about the "sinners saved by grace" part of the identity is important. If I am going too far on the road to self-blame, which is inaccuracy in the opposite direction of pursuing high self-esteem, it is important to humanize and normalize the failure. Self-compassion is extending kindness to the self without ignoring failure, recognizing that we are all fallible, and acknowledging that to fail is to be human.[1] Daily, we need to put our identity

---

[1]Kristin D. Neff, "Self-Compassion, Self-Esteem, and Well-Being," *Social and Personality Psychology Compass* 5, no. 1 (2011): 1-12.

in the proper perspective by thinking about the nature of God, the self relative to God, and then the self relative to others. We are all sinners saved by grace. We are going to fail, but we are already redeemed. This is the buffer against self-pity. Experiments and correlational studies on self-compassion have linked it to nearly every possible positive outcome in terms of mental health and physical health. People who practice self-compassion are more optimistic, happy, curious, wise, and have more meaningful social relationships. Further, self-compassion is negatively correlated with depression, anxiety, and shame, and has demonstrated a positive effect in reducing the symptoms of PTSD.[2]

Establishing the central features of the self as failure-resistant to avoid self-serving bias, and the proper positioning of the self relative to God and others will not end bias, but doing so is part of reducing bias. We need to both establish secure self-esteem and practice self-compassion. These two are connected to the idea that my identity is secure as a child of God, and that I must regularly acknowledge that I am a sinner saved by grace who is worthy of self-compassion. If I don't need to filter information through a lens to affirm the self because I have a secure self-identity, and I'm not spending resources ruminating on failures when I can't bend information to fit a positive self narrative, then I am more open to pursuing accuracy because I have reduced these biasing self-serving motivations.

I am not unbiased. Neither are you. Maybe we can be less biased if we activate our accurate identities as children of God and sinners saved by grace. I pray that we can.

CLOSING PRAYER

Source of all truth, help me to hunger for truth, even if it upsets, modifies, or overturns what I already think is true. Guide me into all the truth I can bear,

---

[2]Neff, "Self-Compassion, Self-Esteem, and Well-Being."

and stretch me to bear more, so that I may always choose the whole truth—even with disruption—over half-truths with self-deceptions. Grant me passion to follow wisdom wherever it leads.[3]

Thank you, God, for the promise that with the faith you have given us we can look at ourselves with sober judgment (Romans 12:3). May we embrace that faith. Amen.

---

[3]Brian McLaren, "Confirmation Bias," in *Practices for Learning How to See*, June 4, 2021, Center for Action and Contemplation, podcast.

INDEX